GODPRINTS

Bible

A GAGGLE OF Giggles and Games

CURRICULUM CENTER
BENNER LIBRARY
OLIVET NAZARENE UNIVERSITY

DISCARD

FOREWORD BY
Lois Keffer

A Gaggle of Giggles and Games

©2002 by Cook Communications Ministries
All rights reserved. No part of this book may be reproduced without written permission, except for brief quotations in books and critical reviews. For information, write Cook Communications Ministries, 4050 Lee Vance View, Colorado Springs, CO 80918.

First printing 2002
1 2 3 4 5 6 7 8 9 10   07 06 05 04 03 02
Printed in the United States of America

Edited by: Jodi Hoch, Lois Keffer and Susan Martins Miller

Written by: Linda Anderson, Mary Grace Becker, Donna Berg, Guinevere Durham, Wendell Garrison, Marianne Hering, Laure Herlinger, Carol Kotlarczyk, Steve Parolini, Jan Pendergrass, Beth Pippin, Dawn Renee Weary, Kristin Wenger, Carla Williams, Pam Mens Wolf, Meredith Wood

Art Direction: Mike Riester
Cover Design: Peter Schmidt, Granite Design
Interior Design: Dana Sherrer, iDesignEtc.
Illustrations: Aline Heiser

Unless otherwise noted, Scripture quotations are taken from the Holy Bible: New International Readers' Version®. Copyright© 1998 by International Bible Society. Used by permission of Zondervan Publishing House. All rights reserved.

ISBN: 0781438403

DISCARD

CC 11464

TABLE OF CONTENTS

CHAPTER 1: COOPERATIVE GAMES

Beach Blanket Party Poppers **8**
Hope on a Rope Tag **9**
Tick-Tock, Roll and Rock **10**
Whatever Floats Your Boat **11**
Flying Tails **12**
Toeriffic Scramble **14**
Toothpick Pictures **15**
Thin Trust **16**
Pull the Pin **17**
Risk and Rearrange **19**
Motion Machines **20**
Extra! Extra! **21**
Criss-Cross Craziness **23**
Shell Seekers **24**
Slipper Spotlight **25**
Not Me, Couldn't Be **26**
Marble Madness **27**
Awesome to Zoorific **29**
Hit the Mark **30**
Flighty Feathers **31**

CHAPTER 2: ICEBREAKERS

Snatch and Attach **34**
Feathered Frenzy **35**
Hot Potato! **37**
Grab 'Em Up **38**
Hooked on Each Other **39**
Off with Your—Hat! **40**
Barnyard Roundup **41**
Zoo Zoomers **43**
Beanbag Butterfingers **44**
Colorful Community **46**
Friendship Web **47**
Peanut Butter Jelly Names **48**
Stick 'Em Up, Or Down! **50**
Toe-tally Slimy Class Pass **51**
A Mile in My Shoes **52**
Don't "Leaf" Me Alone **53**
Monkey in the Mirror **55**
The Great Exchange Game **56**
What's It Worth? **57**
I'm Caring, Orange You? **58**

CHAPTER 3: ROWDY GAMES

Hallelujah Hula tag 62
Beach Ball Bowling 63
"Egg-cellent" Adventure 64
Search for the Lost Coin 66
Balloon Busters. 67
Bug Me! 68
Let's Roll! 69
Songs and Shields! 70
All-Around Roll 72
Faith, Hope, and G'love 73
Vote for Me 74
"Squirt the Shirt" Jamboree 75
Stomping Good Time 77
The Great Garbage Game 78
Get, Get, Give! 79
Pass the Cube 80
Splash and Dash. 81
Lemon Fresh!. 83
Smash and Dash. 84
Fish with Altitude 85

CHAPTER 4: BIBLE MEMORY GAMES

Pull My String 88
Roll 'Em Out Race 89
Undercover Verse 90
Chalk One Up for God! 92
Untangle Selfishness. 93
Counting Clues 94
S.W.A.T (Score With A Tap). 95
Power Puff Praise 96
Square Off 98
Outrageous Obstacle Course. 99
Towel of Blabbing On 100
Quicksand 101
Potato Bud 102
Memory Laundry 103
Sonshine and Raindrops 104
Ra-Ra-Ree. 106
Bibleary 107
God is Eggs-ellent!. 108
Gridsome Journey 109

Index of Godprints and Selected Stories 111
Index of Bible Verses. 112

And all the people went up after him, playing flutes and rejoicing greatly, so that the ground shook with the sound. 1 Kings 1:40

Sometimes the joy of leading children in their walk with God is a ground-shaking experience! If you've been in children's ministry long, you're well aware of the fact that God didn't make young bodies to thrive on sitting still! God built incredible energy into growing bodies. And he gave kids an innate longing to interact with others. Games fulfill so many of those needs! And they fill time and keep the "troops" happy. But are games really the best use of valuable children's ministry time?

You bet—*if* they're thoughtfully prepared to teach as well as entertain. Think of how few hours you have in a week to invest in Christian discipleship with the kids in your ministry. You certainly don't want to pare off a big portion with sixteen versions of Duck, Duck, Goose! But games specifically designed to teach can make a lasting impact. In fact, kids' long-term memory really gets into gear while their bodies are active and happy feelings are pumping through their systems!

The games in this book do far more than give busy young bodies something to do. Each game offers a "Coaching Character" section that's based solidly on Scripture. This kind of thoughtful processing is the key to learning that changes lives. Give kids a memorable activity, then gather them to explore great truths that wrap the activity with meaning and relevance to their everyday lives.

Of course, you're not always looking for a game that has the entire population of your children's program bouncing off the walls! That's why we've given you four different types of games:

- Cooperative Games that get kids working together to accomplish something they can all celebrate.
- Ice Breakers that help kids build community by getting to know each other better without letting up on fun.
- Rowdy Games that use that physical energy that you wish you could bottle to teach memorable faith lessons!
- Bible Memory Games to help kids hide God's Word in their hearts. You can adapt these games to teach any Bible verse.

A Game Closet can make games easier for everyone on your children's ministry team. So grab some Bibles, then stock up on some basic supplies and you'll be ready to go with a game even on quick notice. Here's a list that will get you out of the gate with many of the games in this book.

- Aluminum foil
- Bandannas
- Bathroom tissue
- Beach balls
- Bean bags
- Balloons
- Blankets
- Boxes of all sizes and shapes
- Bubble mix
- Buckets
- Chenille Wire
- Clothespins
- Crepe paper
- Fishnet
- Flashlights
- Frisbees™
- Golf balls
- Grocery sacks
- Hats

- Hula Hoops®
- Lunch sacks
- Marbles
- Masking tape—lots of it!
- Milk jugs
- Mirrors
- Newspaper
- Paper towels
- Plastic garbage bags
- Seashells
- Spray bottles
- Sponges
- Socks
- Tennis balls
- Toothpicks
- Tubs of all sizes and shapes
- Yarn
- 2x4 boards

All the editors of the Godprints team have worked together to bring you a treasury of games that you'll turn to again and again. In this collection, you'll find a game to meet any need—whether it's helping a new group of children get to know each other or reinforcing a key Bible story.

It's a privilege to partner with you. God bless you in your ministry to kids!

Lois Keffer
and the Godprints Team: Jodi Hoch, Susan Martins Miller, Dawn Renee Weary and Mary Grace Becker

BEACH BLANKET PARTY POPPERS!

Make the right choice with an old blanket and some playground balls! Cooperative behavior is a good first step in demonstrating choices that show integrity.

Ages: K and up

Time: 10 minutes

Group size: 6-8

Indoor

Activity level: 2

Noise Meter: 2

Godprint:
Integrity

....

USE THIS GAME WITH:

• God establishes his kingdom forever through David, Psalm 89:19–29, 35–37 (*David demonstrates integrity when he makes godly choices*).

• Building the wall, Nehemiah 3 (*Ezra and Nehemiah show integrity when they work together to build the wall*).

THE GET LIST

• blanket
• scissors
• 3 kickballs

Optional:
• Beach party music and CD player
• blindfolds

STARTING LINE

Cut a hole in the center of the blanket just large enough for one ball to fit through. Then place the balls under the blanket and gather your kids around it.

Welcome to Beach Blanket Party Poppers. Everyone loves a comfy old blanket, so gather 'round! Spread the blanket out and have kids kneel around the edge. **Imagine that we're getting ready for a party and we've spread the blanket on a nice warm, sandy beach.**

But we have a problem. See all the bumps and lumps underneath the blanket? Some of our beach party pals are stuck under there. Our job is to help them pop through the hole in the blanket so they can join the party.

It isn't as easy as it sounds. Without cooperation you won't get far. So work together. When a "head" pops out, I'd like everyone to shout, "Party popper!" Then toss the ball all the way around the circle.

Play until kids have popped all the balls from under the blanket. To play another way, use balls of different sizes. Or use balloons and challenge kids to get them through the hole without popping them. Play another round with blindfolds.

COACHING CHARACTER

• What right choices did you have to make in order to pop the balls through the hole?
• How did cooperation help "win" the game?

Some games work best with individual effort. But others are just as fun when we work together to get the job done.

• What are your favorite individual games?
• What are your favorite games that need players to work together?

In the "game of life," we need to know how to play both ways—with individual effort and working together. That means choosing to cooperate with and encourage others. Sometimes we have to cooperate with people who aren't on our "favorites" list. But team players work hard to give their "not favorite" people as much cooperation and help as everyone else. That's what God expects from us. Have a volunteer read James 2:22. **It takes integrity not to play favorites and to give everyone a chance. And that's an important part of living out our faith! Now let's play again— but this time with blindfolds!**

SCORE WITH SCRIPTURE

You see that his faith and his actions were working together, and his faith was made complete by what he did (James 2:22).

HOPE ON A ROPE TAG

Hang on to hope! This hands-on-the-rope experience will help kids understand that they won't be disappointed when they put their hope in God.

STARTING LINE

Tie ropes to three separate strong tree branches or three separate pieces of playground equipment that are several feet apart. Use paper to label the ropes numbers 1, 2 and 3.

Ask for three to six volunteers to be "taggers." Gather the rest of the kids into one large group a fair distance from the ropes. Have the taggers position themselves between the group and the ropes.

THE GET LIST

• three lengths of clothesline

When I say, "Hope on a rope," everyone will run and grab onto a rope. Stay away from those taggers or you'll become frozen stiff. If you get to a rope but you're not the first one to grab it, hold the hand of someone who is holding the rope. As long as your hand is touching the hand of someone who is holding the rope, you're safe. Are you ready? "Hope on a rope!"

When all the kids except the taggers are either connected to a rope or frozen, blow the whistle and give the next set of instructions. **Now I will call out number one, two or three. If I call out the number of the rope you're on, you'll have to leave that rope and run to a different one. Also, the minute I call out the number, the frozen kids get unfrozen and can run to a different rope. Remember to stay away from the taggers or you'll be frozen stiff. Taggers, take ten giant steps back.**

Blow the whistle to restart the game. Continue calling out number one and number two, but never call out number three. Once a majority of kids are on rope number three, restart the game with new taggers. Play until the kids realize that rope number three will never be called.

COACHING CHARACTER

• Why did most of you end up running to rope number three?
• Tell me how you knew rope number three was safe.
• If someone else showed up to play this game, what advice would you give?

You learned to trust rope number three because I never called that number. Round after round of the game, rope number three was a safe place for you to be. Do you know what? God is like that. God never lets us down. He is always there for us. When it seems like there are "taggers" everywhere in our lives and we get frozen stiff by worries and fears, we know where to turn.

• What kinds of fears and worries get you frozen stiff?

Ages: 2nd grade and up

Time: 15–20 minutes

Group size: large

Outdoor

Activity level: 3

Noise Meter: 3

Godprint:
Hope

. . . .

USE THIS GAME WITH:

• Paul's shipwreck, Acts 27:13–44 *(hope leads to confidence that God will see you through trials).*

• The angel's news to Mary, Luke 1:26–56 *(we have hope in God's Word even when it seems impossible).*

• What's something you can do to remind yourself to trust in God?

Have a volunteer read Romans 15:15. **From thousands of years ago in Bible times until now, God has never abandoned people who keep their hope in him. Sometimes we find ourselves running from rope to rope. Don't do it! Put your hope in God. He will never let you down.**

SCORE WITH SCRIPTURE:
May the God of hope fill you with all joy and peace as you trust in him (Romans 15:13).

TICK-TOCK, ROLL AND ROCK

Ages: K and up

Time: 10 minutes

Group size: 6–8

Indoor

Activity level: 2

Noise Meter: 2

Godprint:
Creativity

．．．．．．．．．．．．．．．．．．．

USE THIS GAME WITH:

• Rebuilding the temple, Nehemiah 2:17–3:32 (*working together and being creative to accomplish a great thing*).

• Jesus sends the disciples out, Mark 6:7–13 (*working in pairs to spread God's Word*).

What can kids learn by creating a huge picture on the floor? Important lessons about cooperation and creativity! As they "paint" pictures with streamers, kids will learn that imagination and creativity are gifts from God.

THE GET LIST
• crepe paper streamers (one roll for every two kids)
• whistle
• large floor area

STARTING LINE
Explain that the object of this game is to "paint" pictures using streamers rolled out on the floor. Form pairs and give one person in each pair a roll of crepe paper. The person holding the streamers is the tick. The other person is the tock. Make sure kids are clear on who is tick and who is tock.

You're a tick-tock pair. You'll take turns tick-tock-rolling the streamers to each other to help make a picture. The ticker is the one who rolls the streamers. The tocker tears the streamer off the roll and gives it back to the ticker to roll again.

I'll call out a picture for you to create on the floor. You'll have a few minutes to make your picture by ticking and tocking the streamers back and forth.

When you hear my whistle, it's time to switch jobs. When I say "tick-tock, roll and rock" you and your partner can get started making the picture I call out. Ready? Tick-tock, roll and rock a _____."

Call out a variety of subjects for kids to "draw": a church building; a fishnet; a church van or bus; a choir; the face of Jesus; the empty tomb. Encourage pairs to swap colors with other pairs. Call time after a couple of minutes and have kids present their "paintings." Take a picture of the creations if you have a camera handy.

Another way to play the game is to pair two teams together. When you call out "tick-tock, make a flock," the group of four of will work together to roll crepe paper creations on the floor. And if you run out of crepe paper, there's always bathroom tissue.

COACHING CHARACTER

• What did you learn about working together in this game?
• Where did you get the ideas for how to make your pictures?

You are truly amazing kids. Do you know why? You were made by our totally aweome, completely amazing God. And he made you in his image—to be like him. So, like him, you have marvelous imaginations and the ability to be outrageously creative! Even all over the floor!

Another great gift God gave you is the ability to work together. That's a gift that we need to work on all the time. This game showed what fun and beautiful things you can create when you combine your God-given talents with the talents of others. Have a volunteer read Nehemiah 4:6.

• When have you worked together with friends or family on a project that turned out really wonderful?
• How does working together help you accomplish something difficult?

God put his people together in communities so we could work as a team. Working together, we can accomplish things that we could never dream of accomplishing on our own. So always be ready to lend a hand. When you work together "with all your heart," beautiful things happen!

SCORE WITH SCRIPTURE

So we rebuilt the wall till all of it reached half its height, for the people worked with all their heart (Nehemiah 4:6).

WHATEVER FLOATS YOUR BOAT

Kids will discover just how much courage it takes to keep their "boat" afloat even as the "weight" of the "cargo" puts the pressure on.

STARTING LINE

Show the class the small boat or wooden block. Demonstrate how it floats in the large tub of water. **See how our boat floats in the water? Let's see if you can guess just how many pennies we can load on our boat before it sinks.** Ask kids to predict how many pennies they think the boat can carry before it sinks. Take the time to record each child's prediction.

Now, let's make a circle around our tub. I'm going to give you each a couple of pennies and then, one at a time, we're going to add a penny to the boat. If we knock over the pile of pennies, we have to start over. Designate one spot for the person adding pennies. Have kids step to the side around the circle until their turns come around. Pass out the pennies and enjoy the

THE GET LIST

- large tub of water
- wooden boat or wooden block (be sure to test it to see how well it floats with a load of pennies)
- pennies
- fish crackers
- paper
- pencil

Ages: K and up

Time: 10 minutes

Group size: large

Indoor/Outdoor

Activity level: 2

Noise Meter: 3

Godprint:
Courage

USE THIS GAME WITH:

- David and Goliath, 1 Samuel 17 *(courage to face our enemies)*.

- Peter walks on water, Matthew 14:22–33 *(courage to keep our eyes on Jesus)*.

excitement as the boat continues to float with its load getting heavier and heavier. It will become more and more challenging to add pennies without knocking over the ones already on the boat.

When the pennies finally take the boat under, pass the pennies out again and make sure everyone takes a few home. Gather the children in another location for a snack of fish crackers to celebrate the game. If there was a child whose prediction matched the outcome, be sure to give him or her the first snack.

COACHING CHARACTER

- What made it hard to keep putting pennies on the boat?
- Did you ever wish it wasn't your turn so someone else would have to do it when it got hard?
- What made the boat finally sink?

Sometimes we have to do things that make us nervous, or even afraid. What if we do something wrong, and the boat goes under or someone gets hurt? Ask a volunteer to read Deuteronomy 31:6 from a Bible.

- According to this verse, why can we be strong and courageous?
- What does "forsake" mean?
- What keeps your boat afloat when you get weighed down by worry or fear?

The "waters of life" can get pretty dangerous. All the temptations we face may try to "take us down." It takes courage to "stay afloat." With God we can bravely face anything that comes our way.

SCORE WITH SCRIPTURE

Be strong and courageous. Do not be afraid or terrified because of them, for the LORD your God goes with you; he will never leave you nor forsake you (Deuteronomy 31:6).

FLYING TAILS

Ages: 3rd grade and up

Time: 25 minutes

Group size: 6–10

Indoor/Outdoor

Activity level: 2

Noise Meter: 2

Godprint:
Responsibility

"It's not my fault." "I didn't know I was supposed to." "It just happened." Sound familiar? In this game, kids will find out that actions speak louder than words.

THE GET LIST

- clothespins
- 3 or 4 bandannas

STARTING LINE

Before class fold each bandanna in half several times until you have a 10 1/2" x 3" "tail." Then place two clothespins, side-by-side, on one end of the bandanna. Gather your kids and ask them to form a large game circle.

Let the game begin! Sometimes in order to win a game everyone must "pitch in." And cooperation is the key to making it happen.

Hand a clothespinned bandanna to one player. **Start by making eye contact with someone in the circle. Say his or her name out loud, and then toss the "flying tail" to that person. That player will catch the tail and then throw it to another player in the circle. Toss responsibly! Hold the end with no clothespins and toss it gently underhand. When you catch the tail, it helps to catch it by the clothespins**. Play a practice round. It may take a while for kids to get the rhythm needed to play the game smoothly.

Once kids have gotten the hang of the game, add another "flying tail" to the mix! Start it with the same player who started the first one. **Let's see how many "flying tails" you can respond to—responsibly!** With practice and control, your group should be able to keep three or more tails flying at the same time.

COACHING CHARACTER

- What did you have to do in order to play well? *(Pay attention; be alert; toss and catch the right way.)*
- What happened if things got out of control? *(Got too noisy to hear; people rushing and not being careful.)*

The game went well when everyone stayed focused. Each time we added another tail, you had to concentrate more. If you didn't, you might drop a bandanna or making someone else miss a toss. Ask a volunteer to read 1 Peter 1:13.

- What does this verse say we should do? *(Prepare mentally; be self-controlled; set our hope on Jesus.)*
- What's hard about being self-controlled?
- Why is it important to set your hope on the right thing if you want to make responsible choices?

When we act with responsibility, we make decisions in our attitudes and actions that bring honor to God, because we have our hope set on God's grace. He helps us be prepared and controlled for whatever situation we might face.

SCORE WITH SCRIPTURE

Therefore, prepare your minds for action; be self-controlled; set your hope fully on the grace to be given you when Jesus Christ is revealed (1 Peter 1:13).

USE THIS GAME WITH:

- Josiah cleans the temple, 2 Kings 22:1–13; 23:1–6; 23:21–23 *(as king, Josiah set his mind on carrying out his responsibility).*
- The parable of the prodigal son, Luke 15:11–31 *(the prodigal took responsibility for his actions).*

TOERIFFIC SCRAMBLE

Ages: K and up

Time: 15–20 minutes

Group size: small to medium

Indoor

Activity level: 3

Noise Meter: 3

Godprint:
Submissiveness

. . . .

USE THIS GAME WITH:

• Mary washes Jesus' feet, John 12:3 *(Mary submitting to Christ).*

• Jesus prays in the garden, John 17:1–18:11 *(Jesus submits to God).*

Encourage your kids to "toe" the line and "nail" the habit of helping others! Kids will learn that they can put others first and still accomplish their task by working together.

THE GET LIST

• participants' socks
• stopwatch
• bucket
• extra pairs of clean socks

STARTING LINE

Gather the kids in a circle in a large room The larger the room the better! **Knock, knock.** (Who's there?) **Toe.** (Toe who?) **Toe how would you like to play a great game with me? Speaking of toes, I need everyone to take off one of their socks. Keep the other sock on your footsie, please. Now toss your sock into this bucket.**

Hand out clean socks to those who are not wearing any. Have kids sit on the floor pretzel style, close their eyes and cover their faces. Place the socks around the room. Hide some and put others in plain sight. When you're ready, have the kids open their eyes.

When I say "Go!" hunt for your missing sock. When you find it, don't touch it with your hands! "Toe" it back to the circle using only your feet. When you get to your spot in the circle, sit down and put your sock back on using only one hand. When your sock is on, stick both feet into the circle. I'm going to time how long it takes you. Ready? Go!

When all the kids have their stocking feet back in the circle, call out the time. **Great job! Now I'm wondering if your toes can move a little quicker. This time don't just go looking for your own sock, but help each other. Remember, no hands until you're sitting in the circle. Then you can use one hand apiece to get your socks back on. Let's see how much time you can shave off the clock by working together.** Give the kids time to come up with a plan. Then gather the socks and repeat the game.

Announce the final time as you collect the extra pairs of socks you handed out to sockless participants.

COACHING CHARACTER

• What did you have to do in order to beat the clock?
• Which way of playing did you think was more fun—playing for yourself, or working with others? Why?

I noticed that some of you did not pick up your own socks right away but shouted out and helped the people whose socks you saw first. Helping others sometimes means that you set aside your own interests to help the group achieve its goals. Have a volunteer read Deuteronomy 6:18.

Jesus himself taught us how to put others first. He never thought of just himself. He cared for the people around him, and he submitted himself to what God wanted.

Thinking of others doesn't always mean giving up what's important to you. Like we discovered in our game, working together can even help us get to our goals faster. By helping each other and learning to make God's will the most important thing in our lives, we can make the world a better place!

SCORE WITH SCRIPTURE

Do what is right and good in the LORD's sight, so that it may go well with you (Deuteronomy 6:18).

TOOTHPICK PICTURES

What do toothpicks have to do with honoring God? Kids will learn that they can honor God with their words, actions and attitudes as they create stick pictures together.

STARTING LINE

Arrange kids in teams of three or four. Give each team one sheet of black construction paper, toothpicks, glue stick and a game cube.

I have a sticky situation for you. You'll be working in teams to create stick pictures on black construction paper. I'll come by and tell each team what to make in your group picture. You'll have a minute to plan together what your picture will be. When I say, "Stick to it," teams begin by taking turns rolling the cube. The cube will tell you how many sticks you can add to the picture. No one else can tell you where to put them. Only you can decide, so choose wisely. Glue your sticks to the paper. Continue to take turns rolling the cube and adding sticks until I call time. After starting the game, give the teams five minutes to play.

Assign each team one of the following:
- Show a place where families gather together.
- Show an athletic field where people play a sport.
- Show an invention that has made people's lives better.
- Show something that can help you learn.

When the pictures are complete have the kids gather and have each team show its picture. Have the class try to guess what the picture illustrates.

COACHING CHARACTER

- What did you learn from working together in your teams?
- How do the talents of many help with thinking up ideas and creating pictures?
- Which picture shows people honoring God?

THE GET LIST
- toothpicks
- black construction paper
- glue stick
- numbered or dotted game cubes

Ages: 1st grade and up

Time: 10–15 minutes

Group size: 3 or more

Indoor

Activity level: 2

Noise Meter: 2

Godprint:
Resourcefulness

....

USE THIS GAME WITH:

- Solomon builds the temple, 1 Kings 6:1–17; 8:62–66 (*Solomon uses his wisdom to build the temple for God*).

- Joshua conquers Jericho, Joshua 6:1–20 (*Joshua honors God by using his skills, creativity and wisdom for God*).

You don't have to be at church to honor God. We can honor God anytime, anywhere and any place. You can honor God by using your skills, talents and knowledge for him in ways that please him. You had to be resourceful to work together and make one picture. Ask a volunteer to read Proverbs 3:13.

• What does this verse tell us can help us use our resourcefulness for God? *(Wisdom, understanding.)*
• Why are these things important when you're working together with other people?

Sometimes we have to make fast choices, and it's hard to be sure we're making wise choices. This verse reminds us not to wait until the moment of crisis to look for wisdom and understanding. If we make a habit of looking for God's wisdom and understanding, we'll be ready to put our talents to use when the time comes.

SCORE WITH SCRIPTURE

Blessed is the man who finds wisdom, the man who gains understanding (Proverbs 3:13).

THIN TRUST

Kids naturally trust things or people they can see. But what about trusting what they can't see? This game encourages kids to break through the trust barrier and land on God's solid ground.

Ages: 3rd grade and up

Time: 10 minutes

Group size: large

Indoor/Outdoor

Activity level: 2

Noise Meter: 2

Godprint:
Trust

STARTING LINE

THE GET LIST

• paper grocery bags
• black markers
• masking tape

Before class, cut down the sides of the paper sacks so they open into long strips. You'll need one for each three kids.

Arrange kids in groups of three. **As a group write the word "Trust" on your open bag and then draw or write some things that people put their trust in.** Give some time for this.

Choose one person in your group to be the truster. The other two will be trustinators. I'll tell you in a minute what your jobs are. Pause for kids to choose their roles.

Trustinators, each of you can take one end of the paper bag. Pull it out so it's flat and straight. Now get down on your knees and hold it so it's about a foot off the floor. Pause and let the trustinators get in position.

Okay, trusters, it's your turn! I want you to step up on to the paper bag. Do you trust the bag to hold you? Do you trust the trustinators to support you?
Some kids may be hesitant at first, not believing that the paper bag will hold them. Depending

on the size of your kids, some bags may tear right away. In other groups, the bag may not tear, but the trustinators will not be able to support the weight of the third person with just a paper bag. All the trusters will end up standing on the floor. Some more resourceful trusters may find a way to support themselves on the other kids and not put their full weight on the bag. That's a perfect example of not really trusting!

COACHING CHARACTER

• Trusters, what were you thinking when you stepped up onto the paper bag?
• Trustinators, what kinds of things did you do to try to hold up the truster in your own strength?

People rely on all kinds of things to make their lives better. What are some of the things you wrote on your bags earlier? Pause and let kids answer. **People think that cars and houses and friends and money will make them happy. But trusting in those things is like trusting in a paper bag!** Ask a volunteer to read John 14:1.

• What does this verse say happens to our hearts if we trust in God? *(We won't be troubled.)*
• Why is it sometimes hard to trust in God?

It's easier to trust in things that we can see and touch. We like to control things for ourselves. God wants us to trust him and not try to live our lives in our own strength. Everything else will fail us just like the paper failed to support us. But God never fails us. When we trust him, we always land on solid ground.

SCORE WITH SCRIPTURE

Do not let your hearts be troubled. Trust in God; trust also in me (John 14:1).

PULL THE PIN

It can be a challenge for kids to learn to sort out right from wrong. Teach the importance of relying on God's wisdom as they learn to be "wise without eyes" and sort what's harmful from what's good.

STARTING LINE

Fill two bowls about half full with uncooked rice. Add 15 of the smallest safety pins you can find to each bowl. Make sure all the safety pins are securely closed. Mix the pins into the rice. Form two groups and choose a volunteer from each group to be blindfolded.

Ask the blindfolded volunteers to tell you about a time when it was difficult to tell right from wrong. **Sometimes it's a challenge to sort things out. What's right and what's wrong isn't always clear. Right now I have something for you to sort out. There are 15 tiny safety pins in the bowl in front of you. Your job is to sort them out and remove them from the bowl. You can't**

USE THIS GAME WITH:

• David faces Goliath, 1 Samuel 17:3–51 *(David didn't trust in the king's weapons).*

• Abraham trusts God with Isaac, Genesis 22:1–16 *(trusting God to provide).*

• Daniel in the lions' den, Daniel 6:1–24 *(Daniel trusted God when things looked hopeless).*

THE GET LIST

• blindfolds
• bowls
• uncooked rice
• tiny safety pins
• timer or watch

Ages: 1st grade and up

Time: 10 minutes

Group size: small

Indoor

Activity level: 1

Noise Meter: 1

Godprint: *Discernment*

use your eyes, but the other people in your group can guide you. When I say "Go!" you'll have one minute to sort out the pins. Then we'll count them and the group with the most pins wins!

Say "Go!" and allow the blindfolded kids to do their best to sort through the rice and pull out the pins. Kids will be amazed that they can't feel the difference between the pins and the rice!

Call time after one minute and count the pins. The group with the most pins gets a 15-second shoulder rub from the team that didn't find as many pins. Then re-mix the pins and rice, choose new volunteers and play again. After several rounds, let the players each take a safety pin to pin to their shirts.

COACHING CHARACTER

- What surprised you about this game?
- When is it tough for you to sort through what's right and wrong?
- Do your friends usually help? Explain.

God wants us to know the difference between what's good and what's bad for us. Like in the game, sometimes we put on "blindfolds" in life that keep us from finding the good things that God wants for us.

- What can keep you from finding the good things God has for you? *(Being too busy; wanting to please my friends; copying the things I see on TV.)*

- What are some examples of things that would help us "see" what God wants for us? *(Positive peer pressure; reading the Bible; praying; listening to parents.)*

God loves us and only wants the best for us. Hold up a Bible. **That's why he gave us this guidebook for our lives. Let's find a verse that will help us understand the importance of this game.** Have a volunteer read Proverbs 15:14.

It's easy to be blindfolded by values and ideas that are wrong because so many people ignore what the Bible says. Unless we're careful to take time to read God's Word and listen to parents and wise leaders who love God, the lines of right and wrong start to blur. God doesn't want us to be blindfolded by what everyone else does. He wants us to open our eyes to the wisdom in his Word. Then we can sort out right from wrong and live lives that honor him. Let your little safety pins remind you to "stick" to God's Word!

SCORE WITH SCRIPTURE

The discerning heart seeks knowledge, but the mouth of a fool feeds on folly (Proverbs 15:14).

RISK AND REARRANGE

Taking a risk can be great fun, but it isn't always easy, especially when it reveals things about ourselves that others might not know. Kids will learn about respect and reverence as they share information about themselves and learn a powerful verse about our awesome God.

STARTING LINE

Create question cards with the questions listed below.
- Who is one of your heroes and why?
- What is the best thing that could happen to you?
- If you could ask Jesus one question, what would it be?
- Who is one of your favorite Bible characters?
- If you could be invisible for a day, what would you do?
- Tell about your most proud moment.
- What animal are you most like? Why?

At the end of each question, write one of the following: Draw 1, Draw 2 or Rearrange. Label one bag *Risk* and put the cards in it.

Label the other bag *Reverence*. Write each word of the following Bible verse on a card and put the cards in the *Reverence* bag: "I will praise you, O Lord my God, with all my heart; I will glorify your name for ever" (Psalm 86:12).

Have everyone sit in a circle. Set the *Reverence* bag in the center of the circle. **Who feels like taking a risk today?** Choose a volunteer and give that person the *Risk* bag. **You, my friend, get to reach into our *Risk* bag, draw a question and answer it.** After the volunteer has answered the question, have him or her follow the directions for drawing cards from the *Reverence* bag. Lay out the words in the center of the circle. Put the *Risk* card back into the *Risk* bag.

Shake up the *Risk* bag and hand it to someone else. **Everyone will get a chance to dip into the *Risk* bag and add to our Bible Verse. During your turn you get to add or rearrange one word of the Bible verse. Let's see if we can help each other guess the right order of the words to create Psalm 86:12.**

For a competitive element, divide your group into teams and provide each team with *Risk* and *Reverence* bags. The first team to complete the verse correctly wins.

COACHING CHARACTER
- What made you willing to take a risk and tell something about yourself in this game?
- As you listened to your classmates tell about themselves, how did you show respect?
- What does the Bible verse you unscrambled teach about showing respect and honor for God?

THE GET LIST
- two paper lunch sacks
- index cards
- pens

Ages: 3rd grade and up

Time: 15 minutes

Group size: 5–8

Indoor

Activity level: 1

Noise Meter: 1

Godprint:
Reverence

USE THIS GAME WITH:
- Hannah's prayer, 1 Samuel 2:1–10 (*even in our deepest sorrow, God's sovereignty deserves our respect*).
- Jesus tells the parable of the place of honor, Luke 14:1–14 (*I can show respect to everyone*).
- Josiah cleans the temple and renews the covenant, 2 Kings 22:1–13; 23: 1–6; 23:21–23 (*God tells us how to live*).

Responding to God and his creation with respect and reverence isn't always as easy as it sounds. Sometimes our feelings and desires get in the way. Our God is an awesome God. He deserves our utmost respect and reverence.

• In what ways have you seen people show a lack of respect for God?
• How can you respond when that happens?

And as God's people we need to show the world what it means to give honor to each other and to God. So take a risk and stand for honor!

SCORE WITH SCRIPTURE

I will praise you, O Lord my God, with all my heart; I will glorify your name forever (Psalm 86:12).

MOTION MACHINES

Ages: 2nd grade and up

Time: 20 minutes

Group size: large

Indoor

Activity level: 2

Noise Meter: 2

Godprint:
Obedience

What could be more fun than creating a human machine? Kids will obey directions, work together and move their machine from place to place.

THE GET LIST

• four carpet squares
• three boxes
• slips of paper
• pencils

STARTING LINE

Label each box with one of the following: hands, feet and free choice. Write three sets of numbers 1–4 on slips of paper. Fold the slips and place a complete set of numbers in each box.

Set the carpet squares about six feet apart, forming a large square with a carpet in each corner. Arrange the kids in four teams, and assign each team a carpet square. Show the labeled boxes to the kids.

You're going to have a blast making a motion machine together. Your team will try your best to make your machine move based on what I call out from these boxes. I'm going to choose a number from each of these boxes. The numbers tell you what can be touching the ground as you link together and move to the next carpet square as a group.

For example, if I choose 4 from the *hands* box, 2 from the *feet,* box and 3 from the *free choice* box, that means that each team must design a machine that has four hands, two feet and three other parts such as elbows or knees on the floor. No other part of your body can touch the floor. When your machine is together, move to the

next square. **When I say, "Motion machine" your team can begin.** Read numbers that you have pulled from each of the boxes. Signal the start. Have the teams design their machines and move to the next carpet square. Make sure all the groups are moving in the same direction around the square. After a brief rest, repeat the game with new numbers and have teams move to the next square. Award points or winners based on cooperation, following directions and team spirit.

COACHING CHARACTER:

• What were some of the obstacles to obeying the directions that I pulled from the boxes?
• How did your team members help overcome these obstacles and follow my directions?

Just as you felt the urge to put out another hand or foot when you played this game, we all struggle from time to time with following God's directions.

• When is it tough to obey in your own life?
• Who encourages you and helps you stay on track?

Have a volunteer read Deuteronomy 26:16. **Christian friends, parents and leaders can remind us to follow God's directions for our lives. When we all work together as a team, we can move forward in God's kingdom. That's why it's great to belong to a group like this! And remember, God gave us the Holy Spirit to remind us of what God expects and to give us the strength to obey. So rely on him—and on each other, and we'll make it through together!**

SCORE WITH SCRIPTURE

The Lord your God commands you this day to follow these decrees and laws; carefully observe them with all you heart and with all your soul (Deuteronomy 26:16).

USE THIS GAME WITH:

Use this game with:

• The Lord rejects Saul as king, 1 Samuel 15:1–34 *(Saul disobeyed Gods instructions)*.

• Noah builds the ark, Genesis 6:9–9:17 *(Noah's obedience meant protection from the flood)*.

Give kids permission to shout—the good news, that is! They'll express an enthusiastic attitude about the job of telling others about Jesus.

STARTING LINE

Pair up the children. Give each pair a newspaper, a marker and some tape. **Good news, good news, read all about it! The front page of the newspaper shows the most important news stories of the day. Imagine what the front news of the newspaper might have said the day Jesus was born, or the day Jesus died. What would you expect to see on the front page of the newspaper about Jesus today?** Give the kids time to answer. **You and your partner will use the paper to make a megaphone. On the megaphone I want you to write something to fill in the blank to this: "Good news, good news, Jesus _____."**

THE GET LIST
• newspaper
• markers
• scissors
• clear tape

Ages: 3rd grade and up

Time: 20 minutes

Group size: partners

Indoor

Activity level: 2

Noise Meter: 2

Godprint:
Evangelism

. . . .

• The shepherds and the
angels, Luke 2:8–20 *(tell
the good news about
Jesus)*.

• John the Baptist, Luke
3:1–8 *(God wants us to
carry the good news to
everyone)*.

After the kids have finished making their megaphones and have written their messages, collect the megaphones. Have all the kids stand in a circle and turn to the side. They should all be facing the same direction. **We're going to all share the good news today.** Hand every other person a newspaper megaphone. **This is what we're going to do. When I say, "Extra, extra, read all about it," if you have a megaphone, shout out all together, "Good news, good news, Jesus..." and read what is written on your megaphone. Then pass the megaphone backward over your head to the person behind you. The next person will do the same. The whole group will need to work together as you shout out and pass the megaphones.**

COACHING CHARACTER

• On a scale of 1 to 10, how excited did you get about calling out the message on your megaphone? Why?
• What was your favorite message among all the ones you saw?

It can be great fun to share the good news about Jesus. In the game, we heard lots of different ways to tell the good news. Ask a volunteer to read Mark 16:15 from a Bible.

• Who does God want to be telling the good news? *(His followers.)*
• Who does God want to hear the good news? *(Everyone in the world.)*
• What is one thing you like about telling the good news?
• What is one thing that makes you nervous about telling the good news?

Sometimes people are shy or too nervous to tell others the good news about Jesus. We found out in our game that there are lots of ways to tell the good news. God will help you find the way that he can use you. Jesus brings us good news and hope! Tell others all about it.

SCORE WITH SCRIPTURE

He said to them, "Go into all the world and preach the good news to all creation" (Mark 16:15).

CRISS-CROSS CRAZINESS

Kids are full of creativity and energy. They'll have a ball making the most of their abilities and resources as they work together to complete a challenge. Kid will learn that using their gifts for God not only honors him but is great fun as well.

STARTING LINE

Arrange the boards on the floor in the shape of a "+" or cross. Place a line of tape on the floor at each end of the long piece. Have the kids form two equal groups and sit behind the tape in a line, one behind the other.

Everyone take a look at the person in front of you. When I say, "criss-cross," find out what that person likes that begins with a 'C'. For example Cody likes criss-cross cake. Margie likes "criss-cross" candy. Now remember who is sitting in front you. Is it Rachel who likes criss-cross cats? You'll need to remember in order to finish the game. Give kids a few minutes to do this and find out some of the fun answers.

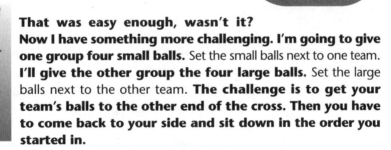

That was easy enough, wasn't it? Now I have something more challenging. I'm going to give one group four small balls. Set the small balls next to one team. **I'll give the other group the four large balls.** Set the large balls next to the other team. **The challenge is to get your team's balls to the other end of the cross. Then you have to come back to your side and sit down in the order you started in.**

But here's the catch. Once you step over the tape line in front of you, you can't touch the floor. You have to stay on the boards. If you touch the floor you must go back to the end of your line. You can only trade places with someone if you're standing on the cross.

Here's the other catch. You can't toss the balls. You have to hand them from one person to another. If someone drops a ball, you have to start it over again from its original side.

Now when I say, "criss-cross craziness," begin. Let's give it a try. When you're finished everyone shout out, "We crissed the cross with craziness!"

You'll need to watch carefully for kids who are following the rules. When they have completed the challenge, make sure the kids are sitting in their original order. Members of both teams may be crossing each other on the board, or they may figure out that if they all work together, and hands their balls to someone on the other team, they will accomplish the task successfully.

THE GET LIST

- 2x4 boards, one long and two short
- masking tape
- 4 large balls (basketballs, soccer balls, etc.)
- 4 small balls (tennis balls, baseballs, etc.)

Ages: 3rd grade and up

Time: 10–15 minutes

Group size: small

Indoor

Activity level: 2

Noise Meter: 2

Godprint: *Community*

. . . .

USE THIS GAME WITH:

- Jesus heals a paralyzed man, Mark 2:1–12, *(using resources to help each other).*

- The parable of the king's ten servants, Luke 19:11–26 *(God helps us to make the most of what we have).*

- The widow's oil, 2 Kings 4:1–7*(trusting God to provide resources that we in turn use for him).*

COACHING CHARACTER

• What was the hardest part about this game?
• What abilities did you use to get this job done?

You had a tricky problem to solve. We started out with two teams, but it was when two teams became one team working together that you solved the problem. Have a volunteer read 1 Peter 4:10 from a Bible.

• What skills and talents do you have that you can use to serve God and others?
• What happens when people work together? What happens when they don't?

God has given each one of you special gifts and talents. Not everyone has the same abilities, so we need to work together and help each other out. When we played Criss-Cross Craziness, you discovered that if you worked together and everyone had a part, you could get the job done. When God gives his people a job to do, he also gives what we need to get it done—including other people!

SCORE WITH SCRIPTURE

Each one should use whatever gift he has received to serve others (1 Peter 4:10).

SHELL SEEKERS

Ages: K and up

Time: 5 minutes

Group size: medium to large

Indoor

Activity level: 2

Noise Meter: 2

Godprint:
Stewardship

....

How do seashells and masking tape teach kids about stewardship? As the kids work together to move their seashells from player to player, they understand the importance of caring for our world's resources and God's gifts. Only by planning and cooperating can they be successful in protecting the gifts they receive.

THE GET LIST

• small clam shells
• 1/2"-wide masking tape
• 2 small containers for each team

STARTING LINE

Form teams of five to seven players. Put separate lines of masking tape on the floor for each team. Have team members sit staggered along both sides of their line. Give all the players a length of masking tape to wrap sticky side out around two fingers of one hand. Place a container with shells at the beginning of each line and an empty container at the end of the line.

When I say "Go," the first player starts passing the shells down the line. You can only touch the shells with your sticky fingers. If you drop a shell, leave it on the floor. It's a dead shell and can't be moved. I'll call time when I see that one team's shells are all either "dead" or in the container at the end of the line. All right, fingers ready? Go!

Watch the teams carefully. When one team's shells are all dead or moved to the end container, call time. Then give kids fresh tape to wrap around their fingers and play again, starting at the other end.

COACHING CHARACTER

• What was the key to moving your shells without dropping them?
• How did you feel when your team dropped a shell?

The dead shells are like things that are ruined in the beautiful world God made. Caring for and managing the earth was the first thing that God asked humans to do. God has given us so many wonderful things to enjoy and use. All he asks in return is that we take care of those things and use them wisely. Ask a volunteer to read Psalm 104:24.

• Have you ever seen something in God's world that's been ruined by carelessness? What was that like?
• What do you do personally to take care of God's world?
• What are some areas of carelessness that you could improve on?

You can be a good steward of the things God has entrusted you with. Just treat all of God's creations as gently as you did the tiny seashells.

SCORE WITH SCRIPTURE

How many are your works, O LORD! In wisdom you made them all; the earth is full of your creatures (Psalm 104:24).

SLIPPER SPOTLIGHT

Kids like to show off what they can do, even if that means not letting someone else have a turn or being unfair. In this game, the person who "slips into humility" will learn a lesson about putting others first.

STARTING LINE

Have the group sit in a circle on the floor. **We're going to slip into a little humility. I will hand out three pairs of slippers. To begin the game you'll have to wait till I call out "Slip into humility." This is what you'll do if you're one to get a pair of slippers.** Take off your shoes and put the slippers on your feet. Then run around the outside of the circle trying to get back to your spot before being tagged. If you are tagged by someone else wearing slippers, you must stop and put the slippers on your hands and finish running around the circle to get back to your spot. If you don't get tagged, just run your little slippers back to your spot. Once you're back at your spot, go inside the circle and choose another person to wear the slippers. But to choose that person you must take off that person's shoes and put the slippers on his or her feet. Then it's your friend's turn to run around the circle.** All the players return to their original spots.

Hand out three pairs of slippers. When you're ready to begin say, "Slip into Humility." To slip in a little more fun, add more pairs of slippers.

THE GET LIST

• three pairs of slippers

USE THIS GAME WITH:

• The Creation Story, Genesis 1–2 *(God gave humans the responsibility to care for and enjoy creation).*

• God the Great Creator, Psalm 8 *(psalm of praise for God's gift of creation to humans).*

• Parable of the shrewd manager, Luke 16:1–18 *(use your resources wisely because they belong to God).*

Ages: 2nd grade and up

Time: 25 minutes

Group size: 12 or less

Indoor

Activity level: 3

Noise Meter: 2

Godprint: *Humility*

• David and Jonathan,
1 Samuel 18–20
*(Jonathan thinks of
David first).*

• Abigail and David,
1 Samuel 25 *(Abigail
takes a personal risk to
save the lives of others).*

COACHING CHARACTER

• How did you feel when you took off your slippers and put them on someone else's feet?
• How did you feel when someone was putting slippers on your feet?
• When did you have to put others first in this game?

Sometimes we feel like taking all the turns in a game, or choosing what we want instead of what someone else wants. To set aside our own interests so that someone else can have what they need is humility. Let's find out what God's Word says about humility. Ask a volunteer to read 1 Peter 5:5 from a Bible.

• What are some ways that we can "clothe" ourselves with humility?
• Who benefits from our humility? *(Others. We do, because God gives grace.)*

In the Slip Into Humility game, some of you might have felt a little embarrassed or silly. But being humble is not about being embarrassed or silly. It's about putting others first and serving them. God doesn't want us to be selfish, but to think of others and put them first. So next time you're feeling a little selfish, slip on a little humility.

SCORE WITH SCRIPTURE

All of you, clothe yourselves with humility toward one another, because God opposes the proud but gives grace to the humble (1 Peter 5:5).

NOT ME, COULDN'T BE!

Ages: K and up

Time: 15 minutes

Group size: all

Indoor/Outdoor

Activity level: 2

Noise Meter: 2

Godprint:
Responsibility

Kids will learn what it means to take responsibility for their own actions, and what it feels like to be accused by someone who doesn't.

THE GET LIST
• one pair of mittens
• a coin or button

STARTING LINE

Tuck a coin or a button in one mitten. Invite the kids to sit in a circle. Show the two mittens and how one has an object tucked inside. Then ball up both mittens like a sock. **Can you keep your eyes on the prize?** Juggle the mittens a bit and ask which mitten has the object. **That was easy, but what if you're sitting in the middle of this circle and these mittens are being tossed "interMITTENtly," or randomly, all around this circle?**

Invite one person into the middle and hand the two mittens to kids at opposite sides of the circle. **When I say, "Not me, couldn't be" start tossing the mittens and let them fly. When I say, "Oh me, oh my," everyone must freeze.** The person in the middle must watch as the mittens are tossed across the circle and overhead, not touching them at any time. Mittens are bound to get dropped, or get thrown to the same person who might mix them up!

When play has stopped, explain: **The person in the middle gets one guess to figure out who has the mitten with the object in it. If the guess is wrong, the group tosses**

again with the same person in the middle. If the person in the middle guessed correctly, the person who had the mitten with the object has to make a choice. Either take responsibility and go into the middle of the circle, or choose to have the person with the other mitten go into the middle in your place! Then start play again.

COACHING CHARACTER

- Who had the hardest job in this game?
- If you had to go in the middle for someone else, how did it feel to get "blamed" for something you didn't do?
- Why is it important for us to take responsibility for ourselves?

Some of you accepted responsibility for having the mitten with the coin and went into the middle. Some of you let others go into the middle. In life, it's not that easy to get off the hook when you've been caught! But we all know that in the long run, taking responsibility for our actions is what God wants us to do. Ask a volunteer to read Acts 24:16.

- Use your own words to tell me what "conscience" means.
- Why is it important to keep your conscience clear?
- How does your attitude affect your conscience?

Even when no other person knows that you've tried to dodge responsibility. God knows. If we keep our consciences clear before God, we won't have to worry that others might find out something we've done.

SCORE WITH SCRIPTURE

So I strive always to keep my conscience clear before God and man (Acts 24:16).

MARBLE MADNESS

Have you ever noticed that when you face challenging situations, you come out the other side feeling closer to those you faced the challenge with? This challenging game will provide an opportunity to meet a challenge with close teamwork as kids try to control a marble with a paint stick and string.

STARTING LINE

Flip the box top over so that the edges are facing up. Put a line of tape across the middle of the box top. Trim each end in the center so you can attach a cup (see diagram, p. 28). Tie two 18-inch lengths of string near the top of each stir stick. Form pairs and give each pair a stick with the two strings attached.

THE GET LIST

- a large box top with high edges
- four marbles, two each of two colors
- paint stir sticks
- twine or heavy string
- scissors
- paper or Styrofoam® cups
- masking tape

USE THIS GAME WITH:

- The parable of the talents, Matthew 25:14–30 *(be responsible with what God gives you).*

- The Crucifixion, the Gospels *(Jesus takes the blame for us).*

Ages: 1st grade and up

Time: 15 minutes

Group size: four players, two per team

Indoor

Activity level: 2

Noise Meter: 2

Godprint: *Forgiveness*

- Zacchaeus, Luke 19:1–10 (*Jesus knocked the sin out of Zacchaeus' life*).

- Prodigal son, Luke 15:11–32 (*the father forgave the son, and the son's life was changed*).

The challenge is to play this game without losing your marbles! Each team will have one side of the game top and one goal. You and your partner will control your stir stick by swinging it from your strings. Together you'll try to get your marbles into your goal cup and keep your opponents' marbles from getting into their goal cup. Make sure each team knows which goal to shoot for and which goal to defend. **The game ends when one team gets all four marbles into their cup. Have a blast trying not to lose your marbles!**

If you want to make the game more challenging, tell kids they can only hit marbles on their own side of the game top, and may not cross over the middle line to stop an opponents' marble or to move their own marble. If no team is able to get their marbles into the cup at the end of a few minutes of play, remove the strings and let them control the sticks with their hands.

COACHING CHARACTER

- What made this game particularly challenging?
- How did the way you worked with your partner affect the outcome?

In this game, like in real life, a good partner can make or break your success in a lot of things.

- Who's been a really good partner to you in sports or in school?
- What makes a good partner?

The most important partner in life you can have is Jesus. He is there to help you through anything. He has what it takes to knock out our sin by dying for us on the cross. His forgiveness is the key to making it to our heavenly goal. Have a volunteer read Romans 3:23–24.

- How can you receive the forgiveness Jesus offers?
- What is it like to have a partner like Jesus to help you meet the challenges life throws at you?

The next time you feel like you're losing your marbles, remember that Jesus is standing right beside you. Hand him the strings of your life!

SCORE WITH SCRIPTURE

For all have sinned and come short of the glory of God, and are justified freely by his grace through the redemption that came by Christ Jesus (Romans 3:23–24).

AWESOME TO ZOORIFIC

Kids will learn to recognize and appreciate the magnificence of God's creation as they work together to name and recall amazing things that God has created.

STARTING LINE

Write the letters of the alphabet on separate index cards. Put all the letters except the letter "S" in a large paper grocery bag. Tape the "S" to the sunglasses. Gather kids in a circle on the floor.

Hey, I have some pretty bright kids in here. I'd better put on my shades! Put on the sunglasses. **These sunglasses remind me of another time I need my shades—when the sun is blazing so hot that little heat shimmers rise from the road. That kind of power is amazing—especially when you think of how far away the sun is—93 million miles!**

Only God could make something powerful enough to give us a sunburn from 93 million miles away! And that's just one of God's amazing creations. Let's think of some other ones. God is awesome because he made the sun. Point to the "S" on your sunglasses and shade your eyes with your hand. **As you can see I already thought of one, the sun.** Shade your eyes every time you say "sun."

Let's see how bright you all really are. One at a time I'll choose someone to pick a letter from the bag. When I choose you, think of something God created that begins with that letter and a motion to go with it. Pick someone to pull out a letter from the bag. Have him or her place the letter where everyone can see it. Then have him or her say, "God is awesome because he made"…say the word and show the motion.

Great job! But this is way too easy for such bright kids. I know, I'll play some tunes! As the music plays you'll pass the sunglasses around. When the music stops everyone freezes. Play the music for a few seconds, then stop it.

Say to the person holding the glasses, **Now you're the bright kid. You get to put on the shades and repeat all the things that God has made. As the game goes on you can all hold up the letters you've drawn and do the motions you made up, but don't say anything. If you're wearing the cool shades, the challenge is to recall everything as fast as you can!**

When the player with the sunglasses gets to the end of the list, draw another card and name a creation that starts with that letter. Then I'll start the music again and we'll see where the glasses end up when the music stops.

Play the music after each turn. Make sure to change the time interval of the music. Repeat until everyone has drawn a letter. Some people may end up drawing a couple of letters.

Be prepared to help kids think of something for difficult letters: Q: quail, quartz, quicksand, Queen Anne's Lace; X: xylophone and x-ray (God gave people brains to invent them!) Keep the pace of

THE GET LIST

- sunglasses
- marker
- index cards
- large paper grocery bag
- CD, CD player

Ages: 3rd grade and up

Time: 10–15 minutes

Group size: small to large

Indoor/Outdoor

Activity level: 1

Noise Meter: 1

Godprint:
Wonder

....

USE THIS GAME WITH:

- Jesus calms the storm, Matthew 8:23–27, Mark 4:35–41, Luke 8:22–25 *(amazement at God's power).*

- Crossing the Red Sea, Exodus 14 *(trusting in God's power).*

- Elijah on Mount Carmel, 1 Kings 18:16–39 *(wonder at the one and only God).*

the game lively with kids flashing their letters and making their motions, and you'll have a hilarious time!

COACHING CHARACTER
• What is one thing that God created that makes you think "whoa, wow and amazing?"
• What part of creation reminds you of God's power?

Have a volunteer read Psalm 68:35. **God is definitely amazing and awesome! No one else is, ever was or ever will be powerful enough to create all of the wonderful and amazing things that God made for us.**

Put on the sunglasses. **It's very "cool" that God is also the source of our power. When you look at all of creation, we're pretty puny little things. But God values us and loves us more than we can imagine. And when we are part of his kingdom, all that power is available for us to rely on.**

• When do you need to trust in God's power?
• Who can tell about a time when God's power helped you get through a challenging situation?

It's just incredible that God is personally interested in each one of us. Next time you face a big challenge, remember—the one who has all the power in the universe is there for you!

SCORE WITH SCRIPTURE
You are awesome, O God, in your sanctuary; the God of Israel gives power and strength to his people. Praise be to God (Psalm 68:35).

HIT THE MARK!

Ages: K and up

Time: 15 minutes

Group size: small to medium

Indoor/Outdoor

Activity level: 2

Noise Meter: 2

Godprint:
Faithfulness

....

How easily are kids distracted by others who challenge their faithfulness? Kids will learn that faithfulness is keeping their eyes on the mark–Jesus.

THE GET LIST
• tennis balls
• poster board
• bucket
• masking tape

STARTING LINE
You'll need three to five tennis balls. The poster board must be large enough to fit over the top of the bucket with several spare inches hanging over the sides. Cut a six-inch hole in the center of the poster board. Attach the poster board over the top of the bucket with tape. Place the bucket in the center of the room. Use the tape to make three circles around the bucket. Make the first circle three feet from the bucket and then make the other two circles progressively larger. Have all the kids stand on the inner circle.

We're going to play a simple game of tenni-ball. It's a lot like basketball, and here's the hoop. Point to the bucket with the poster board lid on it. **Let's see if you can hit the mark. Point to the circle in the center of the poster board.** Hand out the tennis balls to different players. **We're going to toss the tennis balls into the bucket. Before a ball**

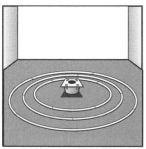

can go in the bucket, it must be tossed to three other players. You can keep track of how many times a ball has been tossed by saying, "Hit" with the first toss. Say "the" with the second toss and "mark" with the last toss. The person who has the ball at that point will try to toss the ball in the bucket.

If the player misses, start the ball again. Each time a ball goes in the bucket move the group back one circle line, so they are getting progressively farther away from the bucket. When all the balls are in, retrieve them and play again.

COACHING CHARACTER

• What kinds of things made it hard for you to hit the mark?
• How do you think you'd feel if you hit the mark every time?

Not being distracted by others but keeping your eye on the mark helped you get the ball into the bucket. Throughout our day it's easy to get distracted by others. They may encourage you to tease someone, take something that doesn't belong to you, or tell a lie. But God has a different idea. Ask a volunteer to read Hebrews 10:23.

• Show me what "unswervingly" means.
• What is the hope that God gives us?
• How does God's faithfulness to us help us be faithful to him?

Being faithful to God is keeping your eye on the mark, keeping your mind set on God. You don't have to do this all on your own. God has promised to be faithful, and he's there to help you do the right thing.

SCORE WITH SCRIPTURE

Let us hold unswervingly to the hope we profess, for he who promised is faithful (Hebrews 10:23).

FLIGHTY FEATHERS

Being fast doesn't always make you a winner. In this game with feathers that weigh almost nothing, kids learn that selfcontrol is the winning track.

STARTING LINE

Divide the kids into equal teams with no more than six players on each team. **What do all these things have in common? Yeast in bread, money in the bank, the turtle in the Hare and the Tortoise.** (The more time they have the better they are.) **Can you think of others things where more time is better than being the fastest or the quickest?**

Give each team two buckets or bowls. One bucket should be filled with

THE GET LIST

• feathers
• music, CD player
• buckets or bowls

USE THIS GAME WITH:

• Peter walks on water, Matthew 14:22–33 *(keeping our eyes on Jesus).*

• Parables of the Lost sheep, coin, Luke 15:1–10 *(God's faithfulness to us).*

• Job, Job 1–42 *(faithfulness to God even in the worst of circumstances).*

Ages: 2nd grade and up

Time: 15 minutes

Group size: medium to large

Indoor

Activity level: 2

Noise Meter: 2

Godprint:
Self-control

USE THIS GAME WITH:

• Esau sells his birthright to Jacob, Genesis 25:27–34 (*Esau didn't use self-control*).

• Daniel eats vegetables instead of the royal foods, Daniel 1:8–21 (*Daniel and his friends used self-control to do the right thing*).

feathers. Place a feather bucket at the head of each team's line. Place an empty bucket at the other end of the room, across from each team. **Let's play a game where it's not always the fastest team that will win. This game will require you to use your self-control. Each of you will have to put one feather on your shoulder or elbow—you can choose which place to put your own feather. Once the feather is on, get to the other end of the room. The object is not to let your feather blow off, fall off or fly off your shoulder or elbow. If your feather does fall off, you must get your feather and start over again. Once you get to the other end of the room, place your feather in your team's empty bucket, then run back to your team. The next team member can go as soon as you tag him or her.**

The team that gets all of its feathers into the end bucket and all the team members back in line first, wins.

COACHING CHARACTER

• What did you find that you had to do in order to get to the other side without your feather falling off?
• How did your team's self-control help you to win this game?
• What would have happened if your team members hadn't used self-control?

In this game, you probably found out that although you wanted to run over to the empty bucket as quickly as you could, if you did actually run, your feather would fly right off. In order to get to the bucket with your feather, you had to walk slowly so your feather wouldn't blow away.

Sometimes life is just like this game. We have a goal—something we want to accomplish. That goal might be to become the best swimmer on the swim team, or to get an A+ on the spelling test. Often our first impulse is to rush right over to get to the goal. That's not always the best way to get there, though. Have a volunteer read Proverbs 25:28.

In Bible times, cities had strong walls around them for protection. If the wall was broken down, the enemy could get in and take control.

• How is a person without self-control like a city with broken walls?

God wants us to use self-control and depend on him to help us do the best thing.

SCORE WITH SCRIPTURE

Like a city whose walls are broken down is a man who lacks self-control (Proverbs 25:28).

SNATCH AND ATTACH

Ages: 1st grade and up

Time: 20 minutes

Group size: 5–20

Indoor/Outdoor

Activity level: 2

Noise Meter: 2

Godprint:
Friendliness

....

USE THIS GAME WITH:

• Ruth shows love and friendship for Naomi, Ruth 1:1–4:12 *(God blesses us when we make loving choices)*.

• The gift of love, 1 Corinthians 13 *(godly ways to care for others)*.

• Good Samaritan, Luke 10:30–37 *(show friendship to those in need)*.

What better way to reach out to new friends than to "pin" them with friendship? Kids will learn that God wants us to let his love shine through as we extend a hand of friendship to those who are lonely and hurting.

THE GET LIST
• small wrapped candy
• clothespins
• envelopes
• pencils
• scissors

STARTING LINE

Give each player an envelope. Set out pencils and scissors. **Before we start this game, I'm going to show you a really neat trick. Here's how to cut two heart pockets from an envelope. I'll cut one from each corner.**

Demonstrate how to draw a heart outline on each bottom corner of an envelope. Show kids how, when the corners are cut out, they make little heart pockets!

As kids cut out their pockets, scatter small wrapped candies on the floor. Then toss a clothespin to each player. **When I shout "Snatch!" use your clothespin to pick up a piece of candy for each of your friendship pockets. No fingers—just clothespins! Ready? Snatch!**

When all the kids have snatched candy and filled their friendship pockets, call them together again. **Set one of your heart pockets aside for later. Keep the other heart pocket and your clothespin. When I say "Attach!" find someone to "pin" with friendship! Use your clothespin to pin the friendship pocket to someone's shirtsleeve, collar, pocket or pant leg. You have 15 seconds to attach the pocket, and you have to pin it on someone who hasn't been pinned already. Are you ready?** Give kids a three count, then shout "Attach!"

When everyone has been "pinned," give these instructions. **Before you can eat the treat in your friendship pocket, you need to find out two things that you didn't know before about the person who pinned you.** Let the kids mix and share, then enjoy their treats.

Okay, one more time. This time you need to pin your friendship pocket on someone else—preferably someone you don't know very well. Ready? Attach! Let kids discover two things about the person who pinned them, then eat the candy.

COACHING CHARACTER

• What fun new things did you discover about each other?
• On a scale of one to five (with one being easy and five being hard), how difficult is it for you to reach out to people you don't know and "pin" them with your friendship?

Have a volunteer read Ecclesiastes 4:9–10.

- Why is it important to reach out to others in friendship?
- Who can tell about a time when someone's friendship was important to you?

God "pinned" us with his love the moment he created us! Make it your job to reflect his love so others may know him and love him. It's easy just to be with the same group of friends day after day, but we all know people who are lonely or hurting and would be glad if we pinned them with friendship. It's not just a good thing to do—it's our job as God's people!

SCORE WITH SCRIPTURE

Two are better than one, because they have a good return for their work. If one falls down, his friend can help him up. But pity the man who falls and has no-one to help him up! (Ecclesiastes 4:9–10).

Plug in the fans and watch the feathers fly! After scrambling for feathers, kids settle into small groups to get to know each another. When you repeat the game, kids also get to practice fairness.

STARTING LINE

Set the fan or fans at an upward angle. To ensure safety, always have adults supervise the use of fans. Mix all the feathers together and put them into one of the grocery bags. If you're going to use more than one fan, prepare one bag of mixed feathers for each fan.

I have a flock of feathers in this bag. I'm going to let the feathers go and when I do, I want each of you to pick up as many feathers as you can. Is everyone ready? Turn the fan on high. Throw handfuls of feathers about six inches from the fan so they go flying everywhere. (If you have helpers to mange other fans, have everyone turn on their fans and release the feathers at the same time.) Turn the fans off when kids have collected all the feathers.

Great job! Now let's take a look at your feathers. Which color you have the most of? Have kids form three groups based on the color of feathers they have the most of.

Now we're going to collect these flocks of feathers back into bags. Hand each group a grocery bag. **Pass the bag around your group. Before you drop your feathers into the bag, tell everyone one thing you've always wanted to do.** Have kids pass the bag and put their feathers into it as they share.

Now I get to pick an honored group. I think I'll pick...the yellows! Give each person in the yellow group a treat. **Now help me re–mix all the feathers and we'll play again.**

THE GET LIST

- electric fans
- large bag of red, blue and yellow feathers
- three large paper grocery bags
- small treats

Ages: K and up

Time: 15 minutes

Group size: at least 5

Indoor

Activity level: 3

Noise Meter: 2

Godprint:
Fairness

USE THIS GAME WITH:

- Joseph and his brothers, Genesis 37:1–28 *(Jacob's partiality toward Joseph causes jealousy and resentment among his brothers).*

- Samuel anoints David, 1 Samuel 16 *(God does not judge by appearance).*

- The prodigal son returns, Luke 15:11–32 *(t he older brother resents what seems to be unfair treatment of the younger brother).*

Start the feather frenzy with the fan and have kids grab all the feathers they can. **Now sort yourselves into groups again based on the color you have the most of.** When kids are in their color groups, have them tell their favorite place to go for fun as they put the feathers back into the bag. **Now for the honored group. I think I'll choose…the yellows!** Give each person in the yellow group a treat.

Then gather the feathers and play again. When kids sort themselves into color groups, have them tell the title of their all-time favorite movie. Then choose the yellows again as the honored group, and give them treats.

You'll probably get protests from kids who haven't gotten a treat yet. Pass out the treats so that everyone receives an equal number.

COACHING CHARACTER

- Was this game fair to everyone? Why or why not?
- Do you think it was important for me to make sure everyone had treats at the end? Explain.

Something deep down inside us wants things to be fair. But you've all had enough experiences to know that "fair" doesn't always happen.

- Who can tell about a time when you saw or experienced a really unfair situation?

God's Word tells us that no matter how many unfair things happen in life, God wants *us* to be fair. Have a volunteer read Micah 6:8.

- This verse identifies three things God wants us to do. What are they? *(Act justly; love mercy; walk humbly with your God.)*

When we show mercy, kindness and fairness to others, we are showing God's love. That can be tough to do if we don't feel that we've been treated fairly. That's when it's important to remember that God shows us mercy, kindness and fairness every single day. It's always fair to treat others as you would like to be treated!

SCORE WITH SCRIPTURE

He has showed you, O man, what is good. And what does the LORD require of you? To act justly and to love mercy and to walk humbly with your God (Micah 6:8).

HOT POTATO!

Friendliness is a lot like a crispy batch of French fried potatoes! The more to go around, the merrier. Have a ball with this lively name game and help your kids start to build relationships that reflect God's relationship with them.

STARTING LINE

Have everyone sit in a circle. **Welcome, everyone! Let's get started with a name game. Before we begin, let's brainstorm a bit about potatoes. You heard me right—potatoes! Fresh or frozen, fried or baked—tell me how you like 'em.** As kids shout out answers, jot them down on the whiteboard. (Examples could include: baked, mashed, French fried, creamed, hash browns, scalloped, twice baked, au gratin, skillet, sweet, chips, tater tots, potato pancakes, etc.)

Wonderful! Now let's get to know each other's names by linking a name with something I've written on the board. For example, when you link mashed potato with Patty you get "Mashed Potato Patty!" Or how about "Tater Tot Tyrone," "French Fry Felicia" or "Boiled Potato Bob?" Take a quick peek at the board and come up with a super potato-name combination for yourself. I'll give you a minute to be couch potatoes and think up your very ap*peal*ing name.

After a few moments, toss the foil-wrapped potato high into the air to get kids' attention. **Okay, it's time for all of us to become "spud buds." Here's how it works. If I toss the potato to you, shout out, "Hello, my name is Baked Potato Paul," or whatever your potato-name is. Then quickly toss the "hot" potato to anyone in the circle and say, "And what's yours?" Then that spud-bud will say, "Hi, Baked Potato Paul, my name is Potato Chip Chris." She in turn will pass the potato to someone new. "Hi, Potato Chip Chris," my name is Sweet Potato Shauna!" Keep tossing until everyone has had a couple of turns. Then we'll open a bag of chips to celebrate!**

COACHING CHARACTER

• Why is it important to learn people's names and use them?
• What's your favorite way to get to know new people?

Jesus was a great example of a loving and friendly person. He looked for ways to connect to others and to make them feel welcome in his Father's kingdom. Have a volunteer read the second part of John 15:15: "Instead, I have called you friends. I have told you everything I learned from my Father." **Jesus wants to be your friend and he knows your name. Through Jesus, people saw the love of the Father. Learning about others and calling them by name is just the first step in connecting with others and showing them we care.**

THE GET LIST

• 1 potato wrapped in aluminum foil
• whiteboard and pen
• potato chips

Ages: 1st–3rd grade

Time: 15 minutes

Group size: 8–10

Indoor/Outdoor

Activity level: 1

Noise Meter: 1

Godprint:
Friendliness

. . . .

USE THIS GAME WITH:

• David and Jonathan, 2 Samuel 18:1; 19:1–7; 20:1–42 *(true friendship)*.

• Priscilla and Aquila, Acts 18:24–28 *(friendliness helps in sharing Christ)*.

- What advice do you think Jesus would give about making new friends?
- As a Christian, how important is it to reach out and make friends with new people?

Keep "chipping away" at the barriers that separate you from people you don't know very well. You never know when you'll make a great friend!

SCORE WITH SCRIPTURE

Instead, I have called you friends, for everything that I learned from my Father I have made known to you (John 15:15).

GRAB 'EM UP

Ages: 3rd grade and up

Time: 10–15 minutes

Group size: medium to large

Indoor

Activity level: 3

Noise Meter: 3

Godprint: *Community*

....

USE THIS GAME WITH:

- The early church, Acts 2:42–47 *(sharing in fellowship and meeting together).*

- A psalm of unity, Psalm 133 *(the joy of unity).*

- Ecclesiastes 4:9–12 *(the benefits of being in community).*

What can kids learn by "sweeping" golf balls across the floor toward a goal? Important lessons about community! Use this name game to help the kids grow closer.

THE GET LIST

- newspaper
- rubber bands
- two dustpans or shoeboxes
- permanent markers
- masking tape
- large indoor space

STARTING LINE

Use the masking tape to make four lines across the width of your playing area. Place two lines about eight feet apart at each end. You should end up with a middle section that is larger than the end sections.

Let's tee-off into some fun as we learn more about each other. Everyone crumple two sheets of newspaper into a tight ball. Wrap a couple of strips of masking tape around your ball, and write your name somewhere on the masking tape. Now toss your balls into this box. Next, let's make bats. Roll up a section of newspaper tightly, then wrap the end with a rubber band. Voilà!

Form two teams and have each team choose a "grabber." Station one grabber behind each end line. The rest of the kids go in the "free zone" in the middle of the playing area. **I'm going to toss all your name balls out into the free zone. You can move around any way you'd like in the free zone. Try to hit as many balls as you can to your grabber. But you can't step into the "no fly" zone—and neither can your grabber. You have to hit the balls all the way across the end line.**

Your grabber will stay in the end zone and use the dustpan to scoop up the balls. When a grabber captures two balls, he or she will call out "freeze." Then the grabber will read the names on the balls. Those people have to shout out two favorite things: their favorite food, and their favorite hobby. Then I'll call out "Thaw!" and you can start batting the balls toward your grabbers again. If there are any balls in the no fly zone, we'll put them in the free zone and try again.

Toss the balls into the free zone and begin play. Continue until everyone's name has been grabbed. Then do a second round of the game and change the topics to favorite book and favorite Bible story. If you play a third round, use favorite team and favorite TV show.

COACHING CHARACTER

Collect all the balls and gather everyone in a circle. **When I toss you your ball, tell us one way that you're a good friend.**

After all the kids have answered, have a volunteer read Acts 2:44.

In the early church God's people shared everything.

• What makes our church a community?

Each of you is a unique person, but because we all share our love for God and each other, we're a very special community. God wants his people to form strong bonds of love and caring. One way to do that is to learn more about each other.

• What's something that you learned about a friend today that surprised you?
• What do we share in our community of believers that's important to you?

On the count of three, toss your paper balls high in the air. Catch someone else's ball. Find that person and give him or her a handshake or a hug!

SCORE WITH SCRIPTURE

All the believers were together and had everything in common (Acts 2:44).

Kid will have fun getting hooked on each other as they learn each others' names.

STARTING LINE

Use the masking tape to mark two circles, one inside the other, on the floor.

Pass out the chenille wires. Have the kids bend the chenille wires around one of their wrists and twist to close. It should make a bracelet with a long end sticking up. Shape the long end of the chenille wire into a hook.

Let's play a game where we get hooked on each other. Arrange the kids in two groups. Position one group on the inner circle and one group on the outer circle. At the beginning of the game make sure the group on the outer circle has one more player than the group on the inner circle. If you have an even number of kids, you'll want two more players on the outer group, or you can ask one of the kids to operate the CD player. **When I start the music, the group on the inner circle will move this way.** Indicate a direction by pointing. **The outer circle will move this direction.** Point in the opposite direction of the inner circle. **When I stop the music, quickly hook up with someone from the other circle. The person who doesn't get hooked will tell us all**

THE GET LIST

• chenille wires
• masking tape
• CD, CD player

Ages: K and up

Time: 15–20 minutes

Group size: medium to large

Indoor

Activity level: 2

Noise Meter: 2

Godprint:
Loyalty

USE THIS GAME WITH:

• Peter is not loyal, John 13:31–38; 18:15–18, 25–27 (an example of not remaining hooked on God).

• Joshua takes command, Joshua 1 (Joshua is loyal to God and his people).

one thing about him or her that we might not know about. An even number of kids will mean you have two kids unhooked and sharing each time. After kids share, have them join the other circle. Have everyone unhook, then start the music again. Run the music for a different length of time for each period of play so that stopping will be unpredictable.

COACHING CHARACTER

• Did you feel loyal to one group or the other? Why or Why not?
• What traits or characteristics do you feel are important for a loyal friend to have?
• How important do you think loyalty is? Why?

When we played the game you might have felt a little loyalty to the first group you started out in. Then your loyalty may have changed to the group that you ended up spending the most time in.

• What happens when you're disloyal?

Have a volunteer read 1 Samuel 12:20 from a Bible.

• How can you use this verse to define "loyalty"?
• How is loyalty to God different than loyalty to your friends?

When you're loyal to your friends, they can depend on you to care about them and stand up for them. Our deepest loyalty goes to God, no matter what our friends think. Get hooked to God in his inner circle and don't step out!

SCORE WITH SCRIPTURE

Do not turn away from the LORD, but serve the LORD with all your heart (1 Samuel 12:20).

OFF WITH YOUR HAT!

Ages: 1st grade and up

Time: 15 minutes

Group size: 4–10

Indoor/Outdoor

Activity level: 2

Noise Meter: 2

Godprint:
Respectfulness

....

Play this game and watch as God's precious children treat "respect" with special consideration.

THE GET LIST

• hats
• a Frisbee™
• a piece of chalk
• treats for all

STARTING LINE

Gather a variety of hats and place them in a box or basket. You'll need one for each player.

I'd like you to look through my hats and pick your favorite one. If your first name happens to have an "H" in it, you go first! Pause as kids pick their favorite hats and place them on their heads. Before they step back from the basket, ask kids to introduce themselves to the group and explain why they chose that particular hat.

Thank you all for sharing. Now off with your head—I mean, hat! Use the chalk to write the word "RESPECT" on the Frisbee™. Then throw or roll the Frisbee towards the center of the

room. Ask kids to form a line 20 feet behind the Frisbee. **Now the object of the game is to take turns (after all, that's the considerate thing to do!) and throw your hat towards the Frisbee. Sound easy? Not quite! If you hit, push or land on the Frisbee with your hat, you're out. Let's see who can come closest to the "Frisbee of Respect" without hitting or pushing it. When we treat others with respect (without all the pushing and shoving), the game is easily won!** If you wish, have kids trade hats and play another round.

COACHING CHARACTER

• How hard was it to get close to the mark without hitting it?
• What happened if you pushed or crowded each other while you were throwing your hats?
• How did treating each other with respect help "win" the game?

All people are precious to God, and he wants us to treat other people with consideration and respect. Ask a volunteer to read 1 Peter 2:17 from a Bible.

• What do you think "proper" respect means?
• How does this verse tell us to treat other people?

Sometimes showing respect means letting someone else have the first turn or the best snack. Sometimes it means showing honor to people who teach and lead us. Sometimes it just means being polite and treating other people the way we'd like them to treat us. The next time you throw a Frisbee—or a hat—look around and see who you can show respectfulness to.

SCORE WITH SCRIPTURE

Show proper respect to everyone: Love the brotherhood of believers, fear God, honor the king (1 Peter 2:17).

USE THIS GAME WITH:

• Abraham chooses peace in separating from Lot, Genesis 12:1–9; 13:1–18 *(we can honor God's call to respect others and live in peace).*

• The "seat of honor" parable, Luke 14:1–14 *(Jesus teaches that we are to value and respect others).*

• Mary anoints Jesus, John 12:1–8 and Mark 14:3–8. *(Mary treated Jesus with respect and reverence.)*

BARNYARD ROUNDUP

The kids will make a joyful noise as they get to know each other by finding their barnyard friends. They'll also learn a valuable lesson about compassion and responding with kindness when others need help.

STARTING LINE

Before game time, put animal stickers on the ends of craft sticks. If you don't have animal stickers, write the names of several barnyard animals on the craft sticks. Make sure you have two of each kind of animal. You'll need one craft stick per child.

Howdy! I'm sure glad you could join our barnyard roundup. I have a cup here with an animal sticker for each of you. When you take your stick, cover it with your hand so no one else can see it. Then peek at your stick to see what kind of animal you are. Before you take your sticks, I need two volunteers to be blindfolded.

THE GET LIST

• jumbo craft sticks
• two sets of farm animal stickers
• large cup
• two blindfolds
• treats

Ages: K–3rd grade

Time: 5–10 minutes

Group size: medium to large

Indoor

Activity level: 2

Noise Meter: 3

Godprint: *Compassion*

USE THIS GAME WITH:

- Ruth, Naomi, and Boaz, Ruth 1–4 *(showing compassion for others)*.

- Jesus washes the disciples' Feet, John 13:1–20 *(Jesus sets an example of how to be kind)*.

- The Good Samaritan, Luke 10:25–37 *(showing compassion towards our enemies)*.

Blindfold the volunteers and have them sit to one side. Let kids take their sticks and peek at them. Then give each of the blindfolded volunteers a stick.

When I say, "Barnyard Roundup!" walk around the room making the noise that your animal makes. Your job is to find your partner by listening for someone making the same animal noise you are making. When you find each other, make sure your sticks have the same animal, then sit down together. When all of you have found your partners, I'll pass out treats.

Point to the blindfolded players. **We have a couple of people here who can't see their sticks. Hmm. I wonder what you're going to do about them. Well, we'll just wait and see, I guess.**

Are the rest of you ready with your barnyard noises? Good! Because it's time for our "Barnyard Roundup!" After a few pairs have found each other encourage them to help others. If no one helps the blindfolded players, whisper words of encouragement to do so. When the blindfolded players have been found by their partners, let them take off their blindfolds.

When everyone is seated in pairs, ask them to hold up their matching sticks. **Wow—it really sounded like a barnyard in here. I'm glad it doesn't smell like one, aren't you?** Pass out the treats and enjoy.

COACHING CHARACTER

- Why did some people need help in this game?
- What would have happened if you hadn't helped them?

It feels good to be kind and help people. Helping people in need is one way of showing God's love to others. Have a volunteer read 1 Peter 3:8.

- How can you tell if someone needs help?
- Who can tell about a time when you needed help and someone gave it? How did you feel about that person?

Be on the lookout for people at home, at school, and in your neighborhood that need help. Try to show God's love to them by being kind and compassionate.

SCORE WITH SCRIPTURE

All of you live in harmony with one another; be sympathetic, love as brothers, be compassionate and humble (1 Peter 3:8).

Kids will learn confidence and each other's names as they enjoy telling others about their favorite animal.

STARTING LINE

Use masking tape to create a starting line and a finish line with a large space in between. Set out chalk and paper at the finish line. Have all the kids stand at the starting line.

Have you ever been to a zoo? If you could be an animal what would you be? Give the kids a chance to chat about the kinds of animals they might want to be. **Now think of another animal that you could be, but this animal needs to start with the same letter as your first name.** Give some examples such as "Bobby Bear" and "Maria Mouse." **Don't tell anyone which animal you've chosen—keep it a secret.**

Now everyone is going to try to get to the other side. Point to the finish line. **You will hop, crawl, run or fly depending on your animal. But not everyone will get to move at once. I'll shout out different things about animals. If I shout out something that fits your animal, you can move. For example, if I say, "has four legs" and your animal has four legs, then you can move like your animal and try to make it to the finish line. But watch out for me, because I might try to tag you!**

If you're tagged you have to go back to the starting line. But there's something that you can do to keep me from tagging you—you can freeze! You'll have to stay frozen until I shout out the next thing.

Invite kids to repeat the instructions to you. **Good—you've got it! Once you get to the finish line write your name on a piece of paper and start drawing your animal. But be ready to drop your picture and go back to the starting line when I call out "Stop it, drop it, back you go."**

As you lead the game, call out the following animal characteristics: wings, antennae, two legs, four legs, eight legs, tail, fur, scales, gills, eyes, flies, runs, makes a web, makes a nest, lays egg, growls, and so on.

When everyone gets to the finish line, give the latest arrivers a few moments to draw, then call out "Stop it, drop it, back you go!" as a signal for kids to put down their papers and return to the starting line. Play three or four rounds, then let kids finish their pictures.

COACHING CHARACTER

Gather everyone in a circle. Have kids hide their pictures behind the backs. Go around the circle and let everyone guess which animal each child was portraying.

THE GET LIST

- masking tape
- chalk
- construction paper

Ages: K–3rd grade

Time: 15–20 minutes

Group size: small

Indoor/Outdoor

Activity level: 2

Noise Meter: 2

Godprint:
Preciousness

....

USE THIS GAME WITH:

- Esther (*God makes special people for special times*).
- Jesus had 12 helpers, Matthew 10:1–12, 40–42 (*I can help Jesus too*).

- Tell me two reasons why you would want to be the animal you chose.
- What's special about your animal? What's special about you?

When it comes to making people, God never runs out of ideas!

- How would the world be different if everyone were just like you?
- What's cool about having all different kinds of people in our group?

We all might look a little different, act a little different and get to other places differently, but God loves us all. Read Psalm 139:14. **God knows what you're like inside and out, and you're precious to him!**

SCORE WITH SCRIPTURE

I praise you because I am fearfully and wonderfully made; your works are wonderful, I know that full well (Psalm 139:14).

BEANBAG BUTTERFINGERS

Ages: 2nd grade and up

Time: 20 minutes

Group size: medium

Indoor/Outdoor

Activity level: 2

Noise Meter: 2

Godprint:
Thankfulness

. . . .

USE THIS GAME WITH:

- The shepherd David, Psalm 23 (*thankfulness for belonging to God*).

- Ten lepers are healed, one is thankful, Luke 17:11–19 (*the importance of giving thanks*)

It's easy to drop the ball, or in this case the beanbag, by failing to thank someone for being kind. What if that someone is God? This lively game encourages kids to practice showing appreciation to those who help them.

THE GET LIST

- beanbags
- Optional: balloons, rice (To make "instant" bean bags, use a funnel to pour the rice into 4–inch balloons. Knot. Stuff the knotted balloon inside another balloon to hide the knot.)

STARTING LINE

Have children stand in a circle about an arm's length from each other. Hand each child a beanbag. Tell the kids to hold the bags in their left hands.

Cross your arms and look at the kids. **Hmm. I wonder who has butterfingers today? Let's find out. Hold your arms out to the side like an airplane with your beanbag in your left hand.**

When I say, "Beanbag butterfingers," open your hand and drop your beanbag. That sounds easy enough, right? Well, here comes the really slippery butter part! As you drop your beanbag, turn to the player on your right, say your name, and catch his or her beanbag—before it touches the ground! If the beanbag touches the ground pick it up and try again.

Allow kids to practice a round before starting the game. **Thank goodness for practice! I saw a lot of beanbags slipping through buttery fingers. Let's all give this a try, but this time if your beanbag hits the floor**

and the person on your left did not catch it, take one step back from the circle and sit out the next round of the game. If the person on your left catches the beanbag shout out, "Thanks, **Ray** (the name of person shouting out his or her name to you), **you made my day.**" Ready? Let's play!

Play several rounds. If kids sit out a round because their beanbags hit the floor, have them rejoin the game for the next round. After each round, scramble the kids in the circle so they get to play with different kids. Remind them to thank all the partners who catch the bags. Then let everyone sit down.

Variation: Widen the circle for more challenging play! After kids have conquered catching the beanbags, have them switch to their right hands.

COACHING CHARACTER

• How did you show appreciation to your neighbor in the circle?
• How relieved did you feel to be able to both drop and catch a beanbag? What made you successful?

Lots of times in life we need a little help from our friends. Sometimes we goof up and drop the ball and other people keep working with us until we get it right.

• Who are the important people who keep working with you and helping you get things right?
• How often do you express your thanks to them?

Have a volunteer read Philippians 4:6. **God knows that we worry about things and that sometimes we let important things slip through our fingers. Aren't you glad that our God is a God of second chances? God never has butter on his fingers, he never drops the beanbag. God loves us and wants to help us. Be thankful! Thank him and show your appreciation throughout the day with prayer and worship.**

SCORE WITH SCRIPTURE

Do not be anxious about anything, but in everything, by prayer and petition, with thanksgiving, present your requests to God (Philippians 4:6).

COLORFUL COMMUNITY

Ages: K and up

Time: 10 minutes

Group size: any

Indoor

Activity level: 2

Noise Meter: 1

Godprint:
Community

....

USE THIS GAME WITH:

• One body, many parts, 1 Corinthians 12:12–31 *(each member of the Christian community is equal and we must work together).*

• Believers pray for Peter, Acts 12:5–17 *(the body contributed by praying).*

If your kids don't know each other well, here's a fun way to get better acquainted. As they combine their multi-colored candy, kids will learn that each person makes important contributions to the body of Christ.

THE GET LIST
• plastic spoons
• Skittles® candy
• bowl
• small poster with outline of person
• marker
• Optional: glue

STARTING LINE

Have kids sit in a circle on the floor. Give each child a spoon. Hold up a bowl full of Skittles® candy.

When I come to you, use your spoon to scoop up one, two, three, four or five candies. You won't be eating these, but we will enjoy some after we work together for a while. Walk around with the bowl and let the kids scoop up their candies. Put three candies on your spoon.

Everyone look at your spoon. How many candies do you have? You're going to share some interesting things about yourself. If you took five candies, you'll tell us five different things. I have three candies on my spoon, so I'll tell you three things about myself. Share three interesting things with the kids. You could tell about family members, pets, hobbies, favorite foods, favorite subjects in school, etc. Then ask each person in the circle to share based on the number of Skittles on each spoon.

Let's use our Skittles to make a mural. Hold up the poster with the outline of a person. **I'd like anyone who has red candies to carefully carry them on your spoon and we'll use them for the head.** Lay the poster flat on a table or the floor and help kids arrange the red Skittles inside the head. Fill in the rest of the sections of the body using these directions.

• **If you have orange candies, carry them on your spoon while walking backwards. We'll put these on the left arm.**
• **If you have yellow candies, carry them on your spoon while hopping on one foot. We'll put these on the right arm.**
• **If you have green candies, carry them on your spoon while walking on your knees. We'll put these on the left leg.**
• **If you have purple candies, carry them on your spoon while skipping. We'll put these on the right leg.**

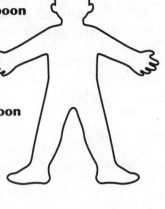

Use the marker to write "The Body of Christ" in the torso section. Pass out extra Skittles for kids to eat while you discuss the Coaching Character questions. Optional: You might wish to glue the candies to the poster.

COACHING CHARACTER

• Tell me one interesting thing that you learned about someone.
• Why was each candy color important for our picture?

Just as we all gave different colors of Skittles to make up our picture, we all come together to make up the body of Christ, worshipping and serving him together. Life would be boring if we were all the same. Some of us gave more Skittles than others, but we all gave everything we had. Have a volunteer read 1 Corinthians 12:27 from a Bible.

• The Apostle Paul wrote this verse. Why do you think he thought it was important to say this?
• What kinds of contributions does the body of Christ need from all the parts?
• What if there were no one to do one of the jobs the body needs?

All of us are different, just like all of these colors are different. But we are all important to God. The body wouldn't be complete without one of its parts. God made each one of us different so we can serve him together.

SCORE WITH SCRIPTURE

Now you are the body of Christ, and each one of you is a part of it (1 Corinthians 12:27)

Together we stand, divided we fall! How better to illustrate the need for connections and friendships with each other than by completing a task that requires players to work together. Kids get to know each other while building a strong and supportive yarn web that keeps a feather afloat.

STARTING LINE

Have the kids join you on the floor in a tight circle. **Who has a holly jolly birthday?** Choose the person whose birthday is closest to Christmas. **We'll all take turns finishing this statement: "I am the happiest when...."** Point to the child whose birthday is closest to Christmas. **And you, my friend, get to start us all out.** Have that child finish the statement.

THE GET LIST
• ball of yarn
• large feather

Ages: 3rd grade and up

Time: 5–10 minutes

Group size: medium to large

Indoor/Outdoor

Activity level: 2

Noise Meter: 2

Godprint:
Friendliness

Great! Now hold on to the end of this yarn and roll the yarn to someone else. Don't let go! Have the person who catches the yarn finish the statement, then hold onto a section of yarn and roll the ball to another player. Each new player will finish the statement, hold the strand of yarn, and pass the ball to another person.

After everyone has received and passed the yarn ball, change the statement to: "It makes me sad when.... For a third round, use "I wish I could...." After the third round, have everyone hold the web tightly and stand up.

- David and Jonathan,
  1 Samuel 18:3–5
  (*Jonathan gave his prized
  possessions to his friend,
  David, so that David
  would be successful*).

- Ruth and Naomi, Ruth
  1–4 (*two friends stick
  together through thick
  and thin*).

Let's see if you have spun enough friendship to keep this feather from touching the ground. If the feather falls through a crack in the web, you'll need to find out some more things about your friends. Drop the feather over the center of the yarn web. Have the kids flap, move or do whatever it takes to keep the feather from falling to the floor as they hold the web tight.

If the feather falls to the floor, have the kids continue playing. Invite them to make up statements to finish. After each statement, drop the feather onto the web again. Keep going until the feather stays afloat. Congratulate the kids on their success.

COACHING CHARACTER

- Tell me something new you learned about your teammates.
- What did you learn about being connected to others when you tried to float the feather?
- Why is it important to develop strong friendships and connections with others?

In the Bible in Romans 12:13 God tells us, "Share with God's people who are in need. Practice hospitality." God wants us to have strong relationships with others. Being a person that others can count on is important.

We can accomplish anything when we're working together. Just like in this game, when we all help each other out we can keep things afloat. But if we don't help each other out, things fall through the cracks. Keep your web of friendships strong and you'll be able to face anything together with God.

SCORE WITH SCRIPTURE

Share with God's people who are in need. Practice hospitality (Romans 12:13).

PEANUT BUTTER
JELLY NAMES!

Ages: K and up

Time: 25 minutes

Group size: 8-15

Indoor

Activity level: 2

Noise Meter: 2

Godprint:
Preciousness

What a delicious way to learn everyone's name. Kids will make a nameplate using peanut butter and jelly cereal. Then they'll have a sweet time playing the peanut-butter-jelly name game.

THE GET LIST

- Reeses® cereal
- Captain Crunch Berry® cereal
- glue
- poster board
- markers

STARTING LINE

Cut the poster board into 4" x 8" strips. We all have something that is special, given to us at birth. Each of has our own name. **Our names are special to ourselves, to those we see every day, to our friends and loved ones, and to God. Let's have a really sweet time with our names.** Hand out the poster board strips. Have kids write their names and glue the cereal to their names.

When the kids are finished making their nameplates, have them sit in a circle with the nameplates in front of them. **Now comes the**

sweet part. We're going to go around the circle and say "Peanut butter jelly." The first person says "peanut." The next person says "butter." The next person says "jelly." Let's see if we can get into a sweet rhythm. Go around the circle once.

Now let's try it again with a new twist. This time after three people say peanut-butter-jelly, the next three people will say their names. Then the next three people will say peanut-butter-jelly and we'll go around the circle repeating the pattern of names and peanut-butter-jelly. Go around the group several times.

Now when I call out the word "sandwich," reverse the direction that the circle has been calling out the names and phrase. Continue to play and randomly call out "sandwich" after someone says "jelly."

COACHING CHARACTER

- Other than your name, tell me something that is special about you.
- What is something that you enjoy knowing about your friends?
- What do you think it would be like if you went to a new place and didn't know anyone?

We all like to know other people, and we like for them to know us. That's how friendships start. We each know people who are special friends. Let's find out who else knows us. Ask a volunteer to read John 10:14.

- Who do you think said these words? *(Jesus.)*
- How does Jesus describe himself here?
- Why is it important for the sheep to know the shepherd and the shepherd to know the sheep?

The shepherd's job is to take care of the sheep. The sheep know who the shepherd is. They follow him and trust him to do what's best for them. That's how it is with God. He knows each of us, and if you were a lost sheep, he would come and find you. You're precious to God just for being you!

SCORE WITH SCRIPTURE

"I am the good shepherd; I know my sheep and my sheep know me" (John 10:14).

USE THIS GAME WITH:

- The parable of the lost sheep, Matthew 18:12–13 *(you are precious to God)*.

- Jesus is our good shepherd, John 10:1–17 *(he takes good care of us)*.

STICK 'EM UP OR DOWN!

Ages: 2nd–4th grades

Time: 15 minutes

Group size: medium to large

Indoor

Activity level: 2

Noise Meter: 2

Godprint:
Respectfulness

. . . .

USE THIS GAME WITH:

- Abraham and Lot, Genesis 12:1–9, 13:1–18 *(Abraham defers to Lot).*

- John the Baptist, Mark 1:1–8 *(John the Baptist was different than most people and valuable to God).*

Kids will learn it is important to respect others and to celebrate that God made us each unique , equally precious to him!

THE GET LIST

- chairs (one for each person in the group, minus one)
- hats of all shapes and sizes (ball caps, sports helmets, ladies' hats, seasonal hats, international hats, silly hats!)

STARTING LINE

Set up two lines of chairs like a train, facing one direction with an aisle in between. Put a pile of hats at the front of the chairs and invite the kids to sit down. **All aboard! Oh, there's no chair for me! I'll show you how I'm going to get a seat on the train. Pay close attention because you might find yourself up here without a seat!**

Choose a hat from the pile and put it on. **First I need to make up a character and say something about that character. For example** (with a funny accent), **"My name is Fred and I like pineapple on my pizza."** Return the hat to the pile. **Now I'll tell you my real name, and you stick 'em up** (show thumbs up) **if you think I really do like pineapple on my pizza, or thumbs down if you think I don't!**

After everyone has voted, explain how you'll show them the answer with your own thumbs up or down. If they got the answer right, they stay in their seat. But if they got it wrong, they have to jump up and change seats. Meanwhile, the person in front grabs a seat, leaving a new person up front. Each time a different person faces the group, he or she must come up with a new character and piece of information to share. Encourage sharing beyond favorite foods, such as number of people in your family, pets, places they've been, and so on. If you'd like to recognize a winner, give a round of applause to the last person to have to get up and change chairs.

COACHING CHARACTER

- Based on what you learned today, who do you think you have the most in common with?
- How many characters were exactly alike? *(Hopefully none!)*
- How hard was it to be polite and still get a seat?

Sometimes it seems as if life would be easier if everyone were just like you! But God made us all different, and each person is valuable to God. When we show that we value each other, we show that we know everyone is precious to God. Ask a volunteer to read Romans 12:10.

- How does this verse say we should treat each other? *(Brotherly love, honor.)*
- What sometimes makes it hard to honor someone else above yourself?

God wants us to be respectful not only to those who are in authority over us, but to everyone. So if we meet someone we don't know well or who is different than we are, we can treat that person with respect. We're all precious in God's sight!

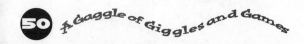

SCORE WITH SCRIPTURE

Be devoted to one another in brotherly love. Honor one another above yourselves (Romans 12:10).

TOE-TALLY SLIMY CLASS PASS

There's nothing like good clean fun with a slippery, slimy bar of soap. Kids will learn more about God's purpose for their lives as they use their toes and a wet bar of soap in an around-the-class pass.

STARTING LINE

Put a bar of soap in a bucket of warm water. Greet the kids barefoot. **Shoes and socks are banned in our game area. So sit down and lose your shoes!**

When kids are barefoot, gather them in a circle. **We're going to have some toe-tally clean fun. When I play the music, start passing the bar of soap around the circle with your toes— no hands allowed! When the music stops, the person holding the soap says his or her name and tells us something he or she likes to do with his or her feet. For example, "My name is Rob and I use my feet to play soccer."**

Start and stop the music so every player gets to share. Good job! You have some talented toes. Now we're going to see how good you are with your hands. The backs of your hands, that is. You have to hold and pass the soap with your palms facing down and the soap on the backs of your hands. This time when the music stops, tell us something you like to do with your hands. For example, "I use my hands to help out my mom at home." Start and stop the music so every player gets to share.

One more time. Now we're going to get your elbows into the act. Pass the soap by pressing your elbows together. When the music stops, tell one thing you've worked really hard at—a project or activity that's needed a lot of "elbow grease." For example, "I used a lot of elbow grease mowing the yard."

If you have a large group, play in two or more circles. When you're finished playing, have the kids wipe the soap off their feet and hands with damp paper towels. They can scramble for their socks and shoes, then rejoin you in the circle.

COACHING CHARACTER

• What did you notice about the things we all like to do with our hands? With our feet?

Have a volunteer read Philippians 2:13. **We learned a lot about each other but there is something to be learned about God, too. God uses the things we like to do to give us purpose in our lives. God has given us abilities and talents to use for him and his kingdom.**

THE GET LIST

- 1 large bar of soap
- bucket of warm water
- paper towels
- music CD
- CD Player

Ages: 3rd grade and up

Time: 15–20 minutes

Group size: large to medium

Indoor/Outdoor

Activity level: 2

Noise Meter: 2

Godprint:
Purposefulness

....

USE THIS GAME WITH:

• Moses in the basket, Exodus 2–3 *(a baby saved for a purpose).*

• Esther to the rescue, Esther *(a woman with a special purpose).*

• Name one way you can use your hands for God. Name one way you can use your feet for God.
• What purpose do you think God might have for your life?

We had some good clean fun, but the point of our game is very serious. God has important things for you to do with your hands and feet. And some of the jobs he has for you might require hard work and elbow grease. You're not just ordinary kids—you're kids with a purpose!

SCORE WITH SCRIPTURE

For it is God who works in you to will and to act according to his good purpose (Philippians 2:13).

A MILE IN MY SHOES

Ages: K and up

Time: 20 minutes

Group size: 5 or more

Indoor

Activity level: 2

Noise Meter: 2

Godprint:
Compassion

. . . .

USE THIS GAME WITH:

• The parable of the Good Samaritan, Luke 10:25–37 *(judging others and disliking them).*

• Jesus raises Lazarus, John 11:1–44 *(Jesus identifies with others' feelings).*

"Never judge someone until you have walked a mile in their shoes." This game allows kids to do just that-put on a strange pair of shoes and do a little walking.

THE GET LIST

• miscellaneous shoes, tennis shoes, high heels, boots, sandals
• 3 x 5 cards
• markers

STARTING LINE

Write one of the following on several 3 x 5 cards: Mom/Dad, younger brother/sister, older brother/sister, teacher, homeless person, grandparent, president, doctor or movie star. You could also use different Bible characters. You'll need enough cards for each pair of shoes that you have. Tuck a card inside one mate of each pair of shoes. Have kids sit in a large circle. Select two to four kids to sit in the middle of the circle.

The kids in the middle will grab a pair of shoes. They'll look at the card to find out whose shoes they have. When I say, "Take a hike," they'll walk around the circle. They'll walk like the person on the card, talk like that person and act like that person, too. At any time if you think you know who the person in one of the pairs of shoes is trying to be, stand and tag the player. If your answer is right, it's your turn to grab a pair of shoes from the pile. If your answer is wrong, sit back down and try again on someone else. The person who was wearing the shoes can join the guessing group. As the game continues either switch names on the shoes or add new ones.

You might wish to ask the kids wearing the strange shoes questions if the other kids are too leery to guess. Sample questions to ask: What do you do? How old are you? How do you feel about….? What was it like when you were a kid? What is a problem you're facing? What's the best thing about…?

COACHING CHARACTER

• What was it like to think and feel and act like someone else?
• Of all the people whose shoes we tried on, who do you think has the hardest job? Who has the most responsibility? Why do you think that?

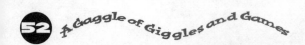

Have you heard the old saying, "Don't judge someone else until you've walked a mile in their shoes?" Sometimes we don't stop to think about how someone else might be feeling or what their problems are. We jump to conclusions. Ask a volunteer to read Matthew 7:1–2.

• What does this verse say about jumping to conclusions?
• What can learn from this verse about trying to understand the feelings of other people?
• How can we "walk in someone else's shoes" at school? At home? In your neighborhood?

God wants us to show that we understand how others feel. One way to understand is to think how another person might be feeling. It's so easy to judge others without getting to know them first. But if we "walk a mile in their shoes," we can better understand them and know how to help them.

SCORE WITH SCRIPTURE

Do not judge, or you too will be judged. For in the same way you judge others, you will be judged, and with the measure you use, it will be measured to you (Matthew 7:1–2).

When you feel blue do you want everyone to "leaf" you alone? This game will get the kids thinking of ways to whirl around in a breeze of kindness to someone feeling a bit blue.

STARTING LINE

Use the green construction paper to cut out many different leaves. Cut one leaf from the blue construction paper. Begin by showing the kids your set of paper leaves. **I have all kinds of different leaves.** Look through and show the leaves to the kids. Then pull out the blue leaf. **I've never seen a blue leaf before, have you? I wonder if our leaf feels blue?**

• What does it mean to feel blue?
• When you feel blue, do you want everyone to "leaf" you alone?

Give the kids time to come up with things that they do when they are feeling down and blue. **Let's see if we can come up with some ideas of what to do when we see someone feeling down and blue.** Give the kids time to brainstorm ideas on how to help others.

Have the children make a circle. Let's pass all these leaves around as I play some music. **When I say "True blue friend," everyone will pass the leaves in this direction.** Point in a clockwise direction. **Whoever has the blue leaf when the music stops must think of something kind to do for someone who is feeling blue. Then that person will pick a friend holding a green leaf. I'll write the idea on the leaf.**

THE GET LIST
• green and blue construction paper
• scissors
• CD, CD player
• marker

Ages: K–3rd grade
Time: 20 minutes
Group size: medium
Indoor/Outdoor
Activity level: 1
Noise Meter: 1

Godprint:
Kindness

USE THIS GAME WITH:

• David and Jonathan, 1 Samuel 20 *(kindness between two best friends).*
• Healing of the paralytic, Luke 5:17–26 *(the friends show kindness by carrying their friend to Jesus).*

If I say, "Someone's feeling blue today," pass the leaves in this direction. Point counter-clockwise. **Whoever has the blue leaf when the music stops will pretend to feel blue.** Have the child walk around the inside of the circle feeling blue. **Then, I'll choose someone holding a green leaf to go up to the blue leaf person and say something to help.** You can tap the child you choose on the shoulder with a leaf. The kids can come up with their own ideas on what to do for someone feeling blue or read the ideas written on their leaves. The game continues until everyone has had a turn to be "blue."

COACHING CHARACTER

• When was the last time you felt blue?
  • Tell about a time when you helped someone who was feeling blue.
  • Name one thing that someone has done to show you kindness.
• How does doing something kind for others make you feel?

Sometimes when we are feeling happy, we forget to look around and see how the other people might be feeling. God wants us to show kindness to others. Ask a volunteer to read Colossians 3:12.

• According to this verse, why should we be compassionate and kind? *(Because we are God's chosen people.)*
• What do compassion, humility, gentleness and patience have to do with kindness?
• How can we "clothe ourselves" with these qualities?

God himself shows us what compassion and kindness mean, because he treats us that way. We have the best example we could ask for to show us how to treat other people. Don't "leaf" a friend in need alone! Whirl a breeze of kindness.

SCORE WITH SCRIPTURE

Therefore as God's chosen people, holy and dearly loved, clothe yourself with compassion, kindness, humility, gentleness and patience (Colossians 3:12).

MONKEY IN THE MIRROR

While giggling over wacky experiences and passing mirrors around, kids will discover a bond of friendship they won't soon forget.

STARTING LINE

Have the kids spread out throughout the room and sit on the floor. Hand out an index card to each child. **What do you see when you look into a mirror? That depends on what you put in front of the mirror. Hold the mirror up to the class. I see a bunch of monkeys. We're going to play a swinging game, where we get to monkey around and learn more about each other. On one side of your index card, in two or three sentences write about one of the funniest things that has ever happened to you—a time when you were just monkeying around.**

Now here comes the really wild part that might drive you bananas. Flip your card over and write your name. But you're going to write the letters backwards and spell your name backwards too. Let me show you. If my name were "Monkey," this is how I would write it on my card. Write the word "monkey" on the butcher paper, spelling it backward and making letters backward.

Have all the kids join you in a circle. Put all the cards in the center of the circle with the names facing down. Hand out one to three mirrors depending on the size of your group. **When I play the music you'll pass the mirrors around the circle from monkey to monkey. When the music stops everyone will freeze. If you're one of the monkeys holding a mirror, swing into the center of the circle and choose a card. Try to guess whose card you have just from the wild and wacky experience you read. Then flip the card over and check it out in the mirror to see if you guessed correctly. If you guessed right, keep the card. If you guess wrong, return the card to the center of the circle.** Play several times. You may wish to give a prize to the person with the most cards.

COACHING CHARACTER

• What's the wildest and wackiest experience you learned about today?
• How does "monkeying around" help you make friends?

Sometimes being with friends can be wild and crazy and lots of fun. When we have fun together, we remember our time together. That's one of the ways that we make new friends. Ask a volunteer to read Psalm 119:63 from a Bible.

THE GET LIST

• mirrors
• index cards
• markers
• butcher paper
• CD, CD Player

Ages: 3rd grade and up

Time: 20 minutes

Group size: medium

Indoor

Activity level: 3

Noise Meter: 2

Godprint:
Friendliness

. . . .

USE THIS GAME WITH:

• David and Jonathan, 1 Samuel 18–20 *(friendship during tough times).*

• Ruth and Naomi, Ruth 1–4 *(strength comes from being together).*

- According to this verse, what's one thing that brings friends together? *(Believe in God, obey God.)*
- What can you do to show friendship to others who believe in God?

When we come together to learn about God together, we share a special bond of friendship. We love God, and we want to follow his ways. Being together can help us do that. Sometimes we're wild and wacky and sometimes we're feeling all turned inside out, like the names in the mirror. Either way, when we come together with friends, we help each other learn more about God's ways.

SCORE WITH SCRIPTURE

I am a friend to all who fear you, to all who follow your precepts (Psalm 119:63).

THE GREAT EXCHANGE GAME

Ages: K and up

Time: 5 minutes

Group size: 6–20

Indoors

Activity level: 1

Noise Meter: 1

Godprint:
Generosity

. . . .

USE THIS GAME WITH:

- Ananias and Sapphira, Acts 5:1–11 *(always give with a pure heart).*

- The Widow's Offering, Luke 21:1–4 *(God loves those who give even when they have little).*

Flowers and candy are popular gifts! This exchange game full of ups and downs helps kids discover that they always have something to give.

THE GET LIST

- plastic flowers
- small wrapped candies
- clear tape
- bucket or basket
- strips of paper

STARTING LINE

On the strips of paper write numbers from 1 to the number of kids in attendance. Tape one to four pieces of candy to each plastic flower. Set the flowers in the bucket so no one can tell how many pieces of candy are taped to each one.

Have the kids join you in a circle on the floor. Each child chooses a number from the bucket. Pull a flower from the bucket. **Who has number one? Have the number one child stand. You may choose any flower you want from the bunch or you may choose this one. After you choose a flower, tell us one thing about yourself and then sit down in the circle.**

The first child sits down. Who has number two? **You may choose any flower out of the bunch, or you may take the flower from the number one player. After you choose, tell us one thing about you.** If person number one's flower is taken, he or she chooses from the bucket again.

The third child can take the flower from any person or may select from the bucket. Continue to play until everyone has a flower. After the kids have all selected gather up the numbers. Have a child draw a number. **Now that everyone has a flower, we are going to pass our flowers to the left.** Pass to the left however many players the drawn number indicates. **As you pass the flower say, "This is my gift to you." When you receive the flower say, "Why, thank you."** Count aloud as the kids pass the flowers around the circle.

COACHING CHARACTER

• Were you ever tempted to take someone else's flower? Why?
• If someone took your flower, how did that make you feel?
• If you had known that you would give your flower away at the end of the game, would you have chosen a different flower? Explain.

The candies on these flowers made them pretty tempting! Mmm. Just thinking about it makes my mouth water. Being generous isn't always easy, but it is what God wants from us. Ask a volunteer to read 1 Timothy 6:18 from a Bible.

• What does it mean to be "rich in good deeds"?
• Tell me some other words that mean "generous."
• How do we do good when we share?

Even if we don't have a lot of money—or a lot of candies—we can be generous. We can be generous by sharing the things that we have, or we can be generous by sharing ourselves with other people. Helpfulness and kindness are ways to be rich in good deeds. And we all can share that way.

SCORE WITH SCRIPTURE

Command them to do good, to be rich in good deeds, and to be generous and willing to share (1 Timothy 6:18).

WHAT'S IT WORTH?

A penny saved is a penny earned, but what is a penny stacked? Your kids will use coins to get to know more about each other and work together as a team.

STARTING LINE

You'll need one bag with a variety of coins in it for each group of four kids. Try to have more coins in the bag than one of your kids could hold in one hand. Have your kids form groups of four, encouraging them to include kids they don't know well.

I'll give your group a bag with coins in it. If you're the first player, reach into the bag and grab as many coins as you can. Then stack up the coins and measure how high the stack is. Then the whole group can help add up the value of the coins. You can keep track of this by writing it on the paper bag. Write your name, the number of coins and the amount of money on the bag. Then put the coins back in the bag and let the next person in your group grab coins.

Kids might think that the tallest stack is the best. But they'll soon learn. The players who happened to grab the most dimes—the smallest coins in size—will likely have the most in value.

THE GET LIST

• small paper bags
• pennies, nickels, dimes
• rulers
• markers

Ages: 3rd grade and up

Time: 10 minutes

Group size: groups of 4

Indoor

Activity level: 1

Noise Meter: 1

Godprint:
Preciousness

USE THIS GAME WITH:

- Creation of humans, Genesis 1:27–30, 2:7, 21–23 *(God formed humans in his image)*.

- Jesus teaches Nicodemus, John 3:1–17 *(God values us so much that he sent Jesus to us)*.

COACHING CHARACTER

- Did the person with the tallest stack also have the most money? Why or why not?
- How do you decide how valuable things are?
- What would you do or buy with the amount of money you grabbed from the bag?

You couldn't tell who had the most money by how tall the stack of coins was. You can't always tell how valuable things are just by looking at them. Ask a volunteer to read Luke 12:24 from a Bible.

- A raven is a bird. Compared to a bird , how valuable are you?
- How does God take care of the birds?
- How does God take care of you?

God values us all, not because of anything we can do well, or because of how we look. We're precious to him because he made us in his image so we could have a relationship with him. We all stack up just right in God's eyes!

SCORE WITH SCRIPTURE

Consider the ravens: They do not sow or reap, they have no storeroom or barn; yet God feeds them. And how much more valuable you are than birds (Luke 12:24).

I'M CARING, ORANGE YOU?

Ages: 2nd grade and up

Group size: any

Indoor/Outdoor

Activity level: 2

Noise Meter: 2

Godprint:
Compassion

Orange you glad we have each other to show kindness and compassion? Use the oranges to engage the kids in "acting out" acts of kindness that show they care. I'm caring, orange you?

THE GET LIST

- oranges (one per 5–6 players)
- thin line permanent markers

STARTING LINE

Have you ever experienced a time when you felt kind of down, maybe lonely or blue? Or things just didn't seem right and it was kind of tough on you? What did you do about it? Let's put our heads together and think of ways that we might help others get through tough times. I'm going to write your ideas on these oranges. Write several ideas on each orange. Repeating ideas is okay, but the more ideas the better. Some ideas include: shake it out like a rag doll, tell them you care, tell a joke, give a hug, smile for three seconds, run in place and count to ten, make a card, and so on.

Many times we can think of really good things to do for someone who is feeling down and blue, but do we really do these things? Let's put all of this caring into practice. Let's show people you're caring. I'm caring, orange you?

Have the kids sit in a large circle and hand out the oranges. Ask a volunteer to read Galatians 6:2. Then have everyone repeat it: "Galatians 6:2: Carry each other's burdens, and in this way you will fulfill the law of Christ." Practice, then have them say the verse aloud as they pass the oranges around the circle. The verse can be said fast or slow. When the verse ends, those holding the oranges must look to see what words are under their thumbs. Have each person read the words out loud. Then have the entire group do or act out what the person said, individually or with partners. For ideas like, "make a card," have the group use hand gestures to make and give a card to someone.

COACHING CHARACTER

- How do you know when someone is feeling down and blue?
- Tell about a time when someone showed kindness to you. Orange you glad they did?
- Name two ways that you can show you care to your parents or someone else in your family.

It's important to reach out to others and show compassion, especially when the "going gets tough." Whether you're at home or at school take time to show kindness to someone who needs encouragement. God gave us each other to help and care for each other. I'm caring, orange you?

SCORE WITH SCRIPTURE

Carry each other's burdens, and in this way you will fulfill the law of Christ (Galatians 6:2)

USE THIS GAME WITH:

- Abraham and the three visitors, Genesis 18:1–8 (*Abraham knew his guests needed refreshment*).

- Ruth and Boaz, Ruth 2:1–16 (*Ruth showed kindness to Naomi and Boaz showed compassion to Ruth*).

HALLELUJAH HULA TAG

Ages: 2nd grade and up

Time: 15 minutes

Group size: medium to large

Oudoor

Activity level: 3

Noise Meter: 3

Godprint:
Resoucefulness

. . . .

USE THIS GAME WITH:

• The parable of the talents, Matthew 25:14–30 *(wisely using the resources you have been given).*

• Joseph is put in charge of Egypt, Genesis 41:41–49 *(Joseph stored up resources for future needs).*

Hula Hoops® and potatoes? Entice the kids in a challenge that will tap into their abilities to be resourceful.

THE GET LIST

• Hula Hoops®
• masking tape
• bucket
• potatoes

STARTING LINE

This game can be played as a large group challenge or in teams of ten players. Use the tape to mark off a starting and ending line, about 20 feet apart. Each team will need three Hula Hoops and a bucket placed at the start line. Set three potatoes for each team at the other line.

All right, all you bright, creative and resourceful hoopsters. You have a mission to save the potatoes! The poor little guys are down there. Point to the potatoes. **As a team you're to get the potatoes from down there into your team's bucket up here.** Point to the buckets.

This is how you hoopsters can save your potatoes. To get to the potatoes you have to use or step in the hoops. You cannot step on the ground at any point unless you're in a hoop. The edges of all three hoops must be touching at all times. You can move one hoop at a time. But the one that's moving can only have two team members in it at a time. Everyone else has to be in one of the other hoops.

I will give you about five minutes to make a plan of action with your teams. I'll also be available to answer any questions you may have. Then when I say "Hula!" your team can start. Make sure players understand the rules and then begin play.

COACHING CHARACTER

• What kind of ideas did you first come up with?
• Did your original plan of action stay the same or change as you played the game? Why?
• What were the resources you had available for this challenge?

The challenge to this game was to think creatively and to use all the resources you were given. God gives to each of us in different ways. Our challenge is to use whatever God has given us to the best of our abilities for his service. Ask a volunteer to read Matthew 25:21 from a Bible.

• What did the servant do well? *(Was faithful.)*
• What did the master do? *(Put him in charge of more things.)*
• What kinds of things has God given you to be in charge of right now? *(Schoolwork, allowance, chores.)*
• What resources has God given you to do these jobs?

Use what God has given you to the best of your ability. What a great privilege to someday stand before God and hear him say, "Well done, good and faithful servant."

SCORE WITH SCRIPTURE

Well done, good and faithful servant! You have been faithful with a few things; I will put you in charge of many things (Matthew 25:21).

This game of shell snatching will bowl kids over with fun. And they'll learn an important lesson about prayer.

STARTING LINE

Place long masking tape lines at opposite ends of the room. Form two teams and have them stand on the lines facing each other. Put the bucket in the center of the room and place the sea shells in it. Give each team three beach balls.

Everyone kneel on one knee. We're going to play a little beach ball bowling. The object of this game is for your team to collect as many sea shells from the bucket as possible.

Here's how to play. As long as you're on your knees, you have to stay still—you can't move forward. So to get to the bucket and snatch a shell, you need to stand up, take three quick steps, then drop back to your knees. Let's practice that right now. Have kids practice standing, taking three quick steps, and dropping to their knees again. **Good!**

While you're moving forward, the other team will be trying to bowl you over. If you're standing or moving forward and you get touched by a beach ball from the other team, you have to go back to the starting line. But if you're kneeling and a ball touches you, you're safe.

When you make it all the way to the bucket, you can remove one shell. Then you have to stand, take three steps and drop to your knees to get back to the starting line. If a beach ball touches you while you're standing with a shell in your hand, the shell goes to the opposite team!

Take a couple of minutes to plan your strategy. Who will be the bowlers and who will be the runners on your team? Bowlers, you can move from side to side, but you can't cross the starting line. The round is over when all the shells reach one side or the other.

When teams are ready, blow a whistle to start the game. After two rounds, scramble the players between teams and play again.

COACHING CHARACTER

Collect the beach balls and shells and have everyone gather in a circle.
In this game, you had to take a risk to go after the sea shells.

THE GET LIST

- masking tape
- 6 beach balls
- bucket
- 5 sea shells
- whistle

Ages: 1st grade and up

Time: 5 minutes

Group size: minimum 4

Indoor/Outdoor

Activity level: 3

Noise Meter: 2-3

Godprint:
Prayerfulness

....

USE THIS GAME WITH:

- Lord's prayer, Matthew 6:5–14 *(one way to pray)*.

- God says "no" to one of David's prayers, 1 Chronicles 22:7–19 *(David's response to God saying "no")*.

- Daniel and the lions' den, Daniel 6 *(Daniel never stops praying)*.

- What are the things you're willing to take a risk to go after in life?
- What do you think being on your knees represents in this game? *(Prayer.)*
- How did stopping to kneel help you?
- How does stopping to pray help you in life?

It's impossible to overestimate the power and protection that God offers to us through prayer. And God wants us to turn to him in prayer all the time! Have a volunteer read 1 Thessalonians 5:16–18.

- How many times a day do you usually talk to God?
- What are some of the challenges you face in life that can "bowl you over"?
- What do you want to remember from this experience?

God is awesome and has given us opportunity to bring anything we want to him through prayer. Don't let life bowl you over. Go to God in prayer! He hears every one of your prayers because he cares for you and loves you.

SCORE WITH SCRIPTURE

Be joyful alway; pray continually; give thanks in all circumstances, for this is God's will for you in Christ Jesus (1 Thessalonians 5:16–18).

"EGG-CELLENT" ADVENTURE!

Kids demonstrate creativity in many different ways. This game sets them loose with their imaginations and God-given creativity to use "eggcessories" for a brand new invention.

Ages: 3rd grade and up

Time: 15–20 minutes

Group size: 4 or more

Indoor/Outdoor

Activity level: 2

Noise Meter: 2

Godprint:
Creativity

THE GET LIST

- bathroom tissue rolls
- tape
- a variety of "egg-cessories" (wooden spoons, new toilet bowl brushes, ladles, wicker baskets, large rubber bands, twine, etc.)
- eggs

STARTING LINE:

If you play outdoors, you can use raw eggs. To play indoors, use hard-boiled eggs. Plan on one egg per group, with a few "egg-stras" available.

Assign the players into groups of four or more. Give each group one roll of bathroom tissue, a roll of tape, one egg and some "egg-cessories." Have the groups spread out.

I've provided you with some "egg-straordinary" supplies. Put your heads together in your group and come up with an "egg-cellent" way to throw and catch your egg.

Create an egg-launcher and an egg-catcher using the bathroom tissue and any of the other "egg-cessories" I've given to you. Each group *must* use the bathroom tissue and at least one other "egg-cessory" somehow.

The trick is this: the egg cannot touch human skin except when you're placing the egg within your launching device! We want to see which group can throw the egg the farthest and catch it without breaking it!

Give the groups ample time to design and create their egg launchers and egg catchers. Have the groups decide which group members will launch and who will catch. When all the groups are ready, have the groups get in parallel lines. The "launchers" should be on one side, the "catchers" on the other. Begin about two feet apart.

At my command, launch your egg. The "catcher" must catch the correct egg (you may want to color-code them with permanent markers beforehand) without the egg breaking to continue in the game.

Have the "launchers" either launch their eggs all at once, or one team at a time, depending on the time and space you have available to play. Each group that successfully catches their egg gets to continue the game, stepping back another foot before launching again. The last team with an unbroken egg wins.

COACHING CHARACTER

• How did your group come up with your idea?
• Tell us how you could improve your launcher or catcher.
• Name one way this game used your God-given creativity.

It's good to use our imaginations. That's how we solve problems—like how to launch or catch an egg, or a new invention that can help people with real problems. God gives us a lot to work with. Ask a volunteer to read Colossians 1:16.

• Where does this verse say everything comes from?
• How did God use his creativity in creation?
• How do you think God can use the creativity he put in you to help others?

Creativity is a gift from God. When we offer our creativity back to God, he can do amazing things through us.

SCORE WITH SCRIPTURE

For by him all things were created: things in heaven and on earth, visible and invisible, whether thrones or powers or rulers or authorities; all things were created by him and for him (Colossians 1:16).

SEARCH FOR THE LOST COIN

Ages: K and up

Time: 10 minutes

Group size: medium to large

Indoor

Activity level: 3

Noise Meter: 3

Godprint:
Self-control

. . . .

USE THIS GAME WITH:

• David spares Saul's life, 1 Samuel 26:1–20 *(David showed self-control when he had an opportunity to hurt Saul).*

• Jesus keeps James and John from acting impulsively, Luke 9:51–56 *(don't make rash decisions).*

What can kids learn by waving flashlights around the room in search of hidden coins? As team members learn to follow the game rules without "bending" them for their own benefit, they'll discover important lessons about self-control and unselfishness.

THE GET LIST

• two flashlights
• 40 coins
• two buckets

STARTING LINE

You'll need to meet in a large room that can be darkened. Place two buckets in opposite corners of the room. Form two teams and assign one bucket to each team. Send kids out of the room while you hide the coins. Hide the coins so they're hard to see without the aid of the flashlight, but not in places that are extremely difficult to find.

Before letting the kids into the playing area, explain the rules and give a flashlight to one person on each team.

When I say, "Search!" you may begin searching for coins in this room. Only one person on your team may use the flashlight. The flashlight has two purposes. One purpose is to help your team find coins. If you find a coin, pick it up and drop it in your team's bucket. You can only carry one coin in your hand at a time.

The second purpose of the flashlight is to "catch" people on the other team who have picked up coins. If you flash them with light and they have coins that have not been dropped in their bucket yet, they're sunk. They have to put their coins in your team's bucket. Now remember, if the other team "tags" you with a beam of light and you have a coin, it has to go in the other team's bucket. To throw in a little more fun, when I call out "switch," whoever has the he flashlight must hand it to another person on the team. Are there any questions?

Play this game for as long as people are looking for coins, or for a set time limit. Periodically, call out "Switch." Watch the game and keep track of those who might not be following the rules. At the end of the game, if you noticed some "rule bending," move coins from bucket to bucket as necessary before determining the winner.

COACHING CHARACTER

• How did you feel when you got caught with a coin in your hand?
• Was it easy to follow the rules, or were you tempted to bend them a bit in order to win? Explain.

Not giving in to temptation takes self-control. That means making wise choices and not being quick to choose the wrong path. That doesn't always come easy, but it's what God wants. Have a volunteer read 2 Timothy 2:22.

• What does "pursue mean?" *(Chase after.)*
• What does God want us to pursue, according to this verse?
• Who else is pursuing the same things? *(All who call on the Lord.)*

God wants us to turn and run away from the things that we know are wrong. And he wants us to chase after the things we know are right. When we're standing in a dark spot, God is there to help us shine a little light on what is right. When we choose self-control over selfishness, we bring honor to God.

SCORE WITH SCRIPTURE

Flee the evil desires of youth, and pursue righteousness, faith, love and peace, along with those who call on the Lord out of a pure heart (2 Timothy 2:22).

BALLOON BUSTERS

What can kids learn by bopping and popping balloons? Important lessons about trust! As they rely on each other to keep the balloons in the air and away from the Buster, they'll learn that God is someone they can always depend on.

STARTING LINE

Blow up twice as many balloons as you have players. Ask all the kids to show you their socks. Choose the person with the wildest and craziest socks to be the Balloon Buster. Give each of the rest of the kids a paper plate.

THE GET LIST
- balloons
- paper plates
- treats

When I say, "Bop n' Pop!" toss the balloons in the air and try to keep them in the air by batting them with your paper plates. If a balloon hits the ground, try to get it back into the air before the Balloon Buster grabs it. If the Buster gets it, he or she gets one chance to stomp on it and pop it. If it pops, the Buster gets to choose another Buster. If the balloon doesn't pop, toss it back in the air.

Hold up the treat. **If half the balloons are left after five minutes of play, you'll each get two treats and the Busters will get one treat. If less than half are left, you'll get only one treat and the Busters will get two treats. So keep boppin' 'n' poppin' those balloons!**

Call time after five minutes, count the balloons and hand out the appropriate number of treats. Have everyone take a few deep breaths to wind down, then gather them on the floor.

COACHING CHARACTER

- What did you trust your teammates to do in this game?
- How do you know whether or not you should trust someone?

God wants you to be the kind of person your friends and parents can trust. Have a volunteer read 1 Corinthians 13:6–7.

- What do you do to show your friends they can trust you?
- What do you do to show your parents they can trust you?

Ages: K and up

Time: 5 minutes

Group size: large

Indoor/Outdoor

Activity level: 3

Noise Meter: 3

Godprint:
Trust

USE THIS GAME WITH:

- Ruth and Naomi, Ruth 1–4 *(Ruth was a trustworthy friend to Naomi).*

- David and Jonathan, 1 Samuel 20 *(Jonathan was a trustworthy friend to David).*

There are Boppers and Busters in our everyday lives. The Boppers are people we trust. The Busters are people who look for trouble. God wants you to be a Bopper—a trustworthy friend who always encourages others. And God wants you to know that you can trust him when something goes bust in your life. When you're a member of God's team, he'll help you keep your balloons in the air!

SCORE WITH SCRIPTURE

Love does not delight in evil but rejoices with the truth. It always protects, always trusts, always hopes, always perseveres (1 Corinthians 13:6–7).

BUG ME!

Ages: K–3rd grade

Time: 25 minutes

Group size: 15

Outdoor

Activity level: 3

Noise Meter: 3

Godprint:
Diligence

....

USE THIS GAME WITH:

• Josiah cleans the temple, 2 Kings 22 *(Josiah shows diligence at his work).*

• Joshua leads the people across the Jordan, Joshua 3 *(Joshua shows diligence and persistence).*

Children work hard to please you. They'll do the same for God! Young children will work hard with sincere hearts when they see God as a game partner. Play the game. Have fun! Then sit under a shady tree and talk about pleasing our heavenly Father.

THE GET LIST

• empty, clean plastic milk cartons or juice bottles
• scarves
• Skittles® candy
• paper
• "jitterbug" music (any fun music will do!)

STARTING LINE

Have enough empty jugs on hand for each child in your group to have one. Before game time, pour one or more large bags of small candies into one of the milk cartons. Have volunteers use the scarves to tie the remaining jugs around the children's waists. Center milk jugs on the back of each child.

Suppose that before I came today I searched your bedrooms and collected all the bed bugs I could find. Shake the milk jug filled with candy. **Noisy little buggers, aren't they!** Hand children the paper cups and fill each one with a small portion of "bed bugs." **Don't eat your sweet and crunchy bugs just yet. You'll need to work hard to give them all away—one little bug at a time. When I turn on the music, walk as fast as you can and try to tag someone. The player will then freeze in place until you drop a "bug" into his or her jug. Work hard to give away all your bugs by the time the music stops.**

Set up boundaries for the game then turn on the fun music. **Now go ahead and bug someone!** Supervise children. Do not allow them to eat while running. Turn off the music to end the game. Have enough candy on hand for snacking after the game.

For hot summer days, fill the milk jugs half full with icy cold water. As kids play "freeze" tag, the water will spurt out the top and cool hard workin' bodies!

COACHING CHARACTER

• How hard was it to tag someone? Did you get tired?
• Did having the milk jug on your back make it harder or easier to move around?
• Did you give away all your bugs as fast as you thought you would? Explain.

I gave you a job to do, and you had to keep working until you got the job done. God gives us jobs to do, too, and he wants us to keep going until the job is done, even if it takes longer than we expect or it's harder than we thought. Open your Bible to Joshua 24:15. **In the Bible, Joshua 24:15 says, "Choose for yourselves this day whom you will serve...but as for me and my household, we will serve the Lord."**

Joshua was talking to God's people, and the people chose to serve the Lord.

• Why is it important for us to choose to serve the Lord? Who else or what else could we choose?
• Tell me some ways that you've chosen to serve the Lord.

God loves hard workers! When we work with a happy heart to do what he wants, God works right beside us.

SCORE WITH SCRIPTURE

Then choose for yourselves this day whom you will serve...as for me and my household, we will serve the LORD (Joshua 24:15).

LET'S ROLL!

It's last but not least on the list of the "fruit of the Spirit" and seems to be a tough one for most of us to handle—self-control. Rolling out-of-control tires help kids discover that self-control takes concentration and commitment.

STARTING LINE

Use the masking tape to make three lines, each 12 feet long and spaced two feet apart. Indicate a start end and a finish end. You'll need to make a set of these tape marks for each team of 10–14 players.

THE GET LIST
• masking tape
• old tires

Each team will need to spread out and stand on the outside tape marks. The center tape mark is where the tire must travel. Set the tires on end on the center start lines for each team. The first players may help keep the tires steady.

When I say, "Let's roll," each team will try to roll the tire down the center tape mark. The tire must stay on the line. If the tire falls or strays from the line, you must bring it back to the start. Everyone will help, trying to roll and guide the tire as it moves on down the center line. But don't get your engines roaring yet. There's more to this game. Nobody can leave the lines. Both feet must stay on the tape marks. Once your hands have left the tire you cannot touch the tire again. And there's no talking. No one can say a word. You may clap, point and jump up and down but you may not make any noise of any kind from your mouth. If you do, the tire starts over. The team that gets its tire to the end first wins.

Ages: 2nd grade and up

Time: 15 minutes

Group size: medium or large

Indoor

Activity level: 3

Noise Meter: 1

Godprint:
Self-control

....

USE THIS GAME WITH:

• Peter's denial of Christ, Luke 22:54–62 *(what happens when we lack self-control).*

• Taming of the Tongue, James 3:3–12 *(self-control with what we say).*

You may wish to try variations of this game. Allow talking, but only one person may speak at a time, and once that person has talked he or she may not talk again. Or only allow one person at a time to touch the tire. Or allow kids to use only one hand.

COACHING CHARACTER

- How hard was it to control the tire as it traveled down the tape line?
- How difficult was it to control yourself (mouth) during the game?
- How did you feel when someone else lost control and the team had to start over?
- How did you feel when you blew it and the team had to start over?

Self-control is the ability to control yourself, especially when you have an urge to get wild and crazy, so that you can do something that honors God. Self-control is not always easy. Don't worry, you're not alone. All of us have problems with self-control. Ask a volunteer to read Galatians 5:22–23.

- Where does help with self-control come from? *(God's Spirit.)*
- Why do you think it's important to have self-control in this list?
- Can you be patient, kind or gentle without self-control? Explain.

The fruit of the Spirit comes from God himself. He wants us to have self-control, and he helps us have it. When we act with self-control, we show that we want to honor God in everything we do and say.

SCORE WITH SCRIPTURE

But the fruit of the Spirit is love, joy, peace, patience, kindness, goodness, faithfulness, gentleness and self-control (Galatians 5:22–23).

SONGS AND SHIELDS!

Ages: K and up

Time: 10 minutes or longer

Group size: large

Indoor/Outdoor

Activity level: 3

Noise Meter: 3

Godprint:
Joy

Trashcan lids and Frisbees? What can kids learn from those? As kids switch positions in this fast-paced game, they'll learn that God protects them and gives them joy!

THE GET LIST

- Frisbees™
- trashcan lids with handles (cleaned)
- crepe paper streamers taped to sticks
- masking tape or colorful electrical tape

STARTING LINE

Tape or tie lengths of crepe paper streamers to sticks. Make one streamer stick for every three players. Use the tape to create a rectangular playing area large enough to encompass your group's size. Put half of the streamer sticks behind one short line of the rectangle and the other half behind the opposite short line. Then place half of the Frisbees behind a long line, and the other half behind the opposite long line. Place the trashcan lids in the center of the playing area. Divide the participants into six equal groups.

Send two of the groups to the streamers at the ends of the playing field. **You're the Songsters! When we play, wave your streamers in the air and sing any praise song you want to— with a loud, joyful voice! You must praise God the whole time you're a Songster.**

Send two of the groups to the Frisbees at either side. **Your Frisbees represent life's trials. You must get on your knees and toss the Frisbees to the other side.** Inform the kids that they must keep the Frisbees down low so that if anyone is hit, it's belly-level or lower. **If your Frisbee doesn't make it to the other side where the rest of the life's trials are, then quickly retrieve your Frisbee, go back to the edge of the playing area and toss it again.**

Send one group into the center of the playing area with the trashcan lids. **You're God's Shields. You protect the runners from Life's Trials. Use your shields to block the Frisbees from hitting the runners.**

Split the last group and send them to both ends of the playing field with the Songsters. **You're the runners. You run around in life, just like we all do. You must run from one end to the other without getting hit by one of life's trials. If you get hit, trade places with a God's Shield person.** The Runner becomes a God's Shield and the God's Shield person becomes a Runner. **If you make it all the way across without getting hit, trade places with a Songster.** The Runner becomes a Songster and the Songster becomes a Runner.

Keep playing until I give a signal. Then we'll switch places so everyone gets a chance to be a part of all the groups.

Play until everyone gets a chance to be in all four positions. Gather the materials together as the participants catch their breaths and calm down a bit.

COACHING CHARACTER

• How did you feel when you were God's Shield, protecting those running around in life?
• When you were a Runner, did you feel you could trust God's Shield to protect you? Why or why not?
• How is this game like real life?
• Tell us why you think God wants us to be joyful in life.

In this game, we learned that God is our strength and our shield. A shield is used for protection; God is our protection! We learned we can trust in God, knowing he will help us. And, just like in life, even when we go through "trials," we still have joy and can praise God with songs. Have a volunteer read Psalm 28:7 from a Bible.

• What does this verse say the Lord does for us?
• According to this verse, how should we respond to what God does for us?
• What does it feel like when your heart "leaps for joy"?

Our game got a little confusing sometimes. Life is like that, too. We can't predict everything that's going to happen. But we can be sure of one thing: God is with us, caring for us no matter what happens. And that's a great reason to be joyful!

SCORE WITH SCRIPTURE

The LORD is my strength and my shield; my heart trusts in him, and I am helped. My heart leaps for joy and I will give thanks to him in song (Psalm 28:7).

USE THIS GAME WITH:

• The various stories of David's life, Psalms; 1 and 2 Samuel; 1 and 2 Kings *(trusting God to help in times in need; relying on God as a source of joy; giving thanks in song).*

• Paul and Silas in prison, Acts 16:16–34 *(trusting God's protection and being joyful in trials).*

ALL-AROUND ROLL

Ages: 3rd grade and up

Time: 20 minutes

Group size: any

Indoor

Activity level: 2

Noise Meter: 2

Godprint:
Perseverance

. . . .

USE THIS GAME WITH:

• Joseph's imprisonment, Genesis 39:20–41:43 *(Joseph remained faithful in the face of many setbacks).*

• Job's steady faith, Job 1, 2, 19:25–27, 42:7–17 *(look to future reward in the loss of worldly things).*

• Paul's hardships, 2 Corinthians 11:23–31 *(boasting in God's strength during times of weakness).*

"Oh no! Not again!" Perseverance means "try, try, try again" while relying on God's strength. That's what kids will learn in this game, as they roll bathroom tissue toward a central goal.

THE GET LIST
• masking tape
• chair
• bathroom tissue rolls

STARTING LINE

Use masking tape to mark a ten-foot circle on the floor. If you have a large group, make a circle for every ten kids. Place a chair in the center of the circle. Assign each player a spot on the circle, and give each player a roll of bathroom tissue

When I say, "Roll 'em," hold the end of your bathroom tissue, and roll the rest of it toward the chair. Score by getting your roll to stop under the chair.

If your tissue breaks, toss the loose part outside the circle and begin again. If your roll stops short of the chair, walk inside the circle and roll up the paper using your nose to push it back!

Some of you may finish early; others of you may have to work at it over and over.

Sometimes I'll say, "Shake, rattle and roll." That means that everyone must roll up the tissue—with your nose, of course—run around the circle twice and find a new spot to roll from.

Take time to answer any questions, and then give a starting signal. Walk around the outside of the circle to see that rules are being followed and to cheer on the kids. Randomly shout out "Shake, rattle and roll."

COACHING CHARACTER

• How often did you have to re-roll your tissue before you reached the goal?
• How did you feel about having to repeat the task?
• What helped you to persevere through the game?

God doesn't want us to be the kind of people who are easily discouraged and quit. He wants a team of strong people who persevere because they know the reward is worth the effort. God promises that he will renew our strength as we rely on him and ask for his help. Ask a volunteer to read Philippians 3:13–14.

• Why is it important to "forget what lies behind" in order to persevere?
• What words in these verses tell us that perseverance is hard work? *(Straining, press on.)*

The Apostle Paul wrote these words. During his life he was beaten, chased out of town, shipwrecked and imprisoned more than once. He knew what it was to suffer and have good reason to quit. But he didn't. He pressed on, because he knew the work he was doing was God's work. His goal was to be like Christ.

- What kinds of things do you have to forget about when you want to keep going at something that's hard?
- What part of our game represented "forgetting what lies behind"? *(Throwing away broken strips.)*
- What part of our game represented "pressing on"? *(Pick up the roll and try again.)*

The next time you feel like quitting, remember your roll of tissue! And persevere!

SCORE WITH SCRIPTURE

But one thing I do: Forgetting what is behind and straining toward what is ahead, I press on toward the goal to win the prize for which God has called me heavenward in Christ Jesus (Philippians 3:13–14).

FAITH, HOPE, AND G'LOVE

Walking backward with their eyes closed helps kids discover they need to trust God to get them where he wants them to go.

STARTING LINE

You can play this with teams or as one large group. You'll need a baseball glove for each team. Have the kids line up with everyone facing the same direction. Players should stand about an arm's length apart.

THE GET LIST
- large baseball gloves

We're going to work together passing this glove over our heads and through our legs to the end of the line. If you get the glove from over your head, pass it back through your legs. If you get the glove through someone's legs, pass it over your head. The glove must be passed in an over-and-under pattern starting at the front of the line to the back of the line.

Once the glove reaches the end of the line, the last person goes to the front of the line. Here's the tricky part: if you're the last person, you have to close your eyes and walk backward to get there. Everyone else can use voices only to guide you. When you reach the front of the line you becomes the first person in line and start passing the glove back again in the over-and-under pattern. When the first person is back to the front of the line, we'll all cheer, "Faith, Hope and G'love!"

COACHING CHARACTER

- How did it feel to be guided to the front when you couldn't see?
- How easily did you get off track when you couldn't see where you were going?
- Whose voices did you hear that you trusted?

When you closed your eyes and couldn't see where you were going, you knew you had some help you could trust to get you to the right place. This game reminds us that we need to trust God, not ourselves, to get through the challenges in our lives. Ask a volunteer to read 2 Corinthians 5:7.

Ages: K and up

Time: 15 minutes

Group size: medium to large

Indoor

Activity level: 2

Noise Meter: 2

Godprint:
Faith

. . . .

USE THIS GAME WITH:

- Noah's Ark, Genesis 6–8 *(belief in the unseen).*

- Paul's ministry in Acts *(faith to overcome trials).*

- Tell me some words that explain what "faith" means.
- In your own words, what does this verse mean?
- Give me some examples of when you need to live by faith.

Sometimes it's hard to trust in God's plan for us. But if we try to do everything in our own strength, we'll end up making mistakes. God loves us and knows what's best for us. Our job is to trust him—live by faith, not by sight.

SCORE WITH SCRIPTURE

We live by faith, not by sight (2 Corinthians 5:7).

Hold this mock election and see who has the strength of conviction to get voted in by their peers as the most convincing candidate. Then, play this riotous game and see which candidate really has the right stuff!

Ages: 3rd grade and up

Time: 20 minutes

Group size: large

Outdoor

Activity level: 3

Noise Meter: 3

Godprint:
Conviction

. . . .

USE THIS GAME WITH:

- Fiery Furnace, Daniel 3:1–30 *(unshakable conviction in the one true God).*

- Elijah on Mt. Carmel, 1 Kings 18:16–39 *(conviction in the power of God).*

THE GET LIST

- **a bucket filled with water**
- **paper cups**
- **blindfolds**
- **a shallow bowl**

STARTING LINE

For each team place a bucket filled with water across the room with some paper cups and a blindfold nearby. At the other end of the room place the empty bowl. Assign kids to two teams.

Explain that each team needs to select a "bowl holder." This person will lie on his or her back with the empty bowl placed on his or her stomach. The rest of the team will take turns carrying a cup of water from the bucket and pouring it into the empty bowl. But they'll be blindfolded as they carry and pour the water. The "bowl holder" will need to direct the blindfolded teammates to the right location as well as keep the bowl from spilling.

Let's find out who will be the bowl holder for each team. If you want to try for the job, you'll have to give a convincing speech about why you believe you should be the bowl holder for your team. Each team will then select a bowl holder. Have the candidates give brief speeches and then let each team vote for a bowl holder.

Place the bowl holder and bowl in position, and line up teammates at the bucket. **The votes are in and we have our bowl holders. When I say, "Dip away," each team may begin with the first player getting blindfolded, dipping a cup in the water, traveling to the bowl holder and dumping the cup of water in the bowl. Once the water has been dumped the player may remove the blindfold and run back to the team to hand off the blindfold to the next player. Once all the players have had a turn the game is finished.** Don't tell the kids, but the fastest team doesn't necessarily get rewarded. The team with the driest bowl holder wins.

A fun option to add is to encourage each team to spend its time trying to make the other team's bowl holder laugh. This may cause the bowl to shake and the water to spill.

COACHING CHARACTER

• What convinced you to choose the candidate you voted for?
• How sure were you that your candidate would be able to give you good directions and keep the bowl from spilling?

Confidence is a funny thing. We may feel confident in one thing, but not confident in another thing. Give an example from your life. **Our confidence belongs in God, not in ourselves.** Read Isaiah 7:9b from a Bible: "If you do not stand firm in your faith, you will not stand at all."

• What kinds of things keep you from standing firm in your faith?
• If your faith is wobbly, what do you think happens to your life?

We can stand firm on the unchanging truth of God's Word. Even when you may not feel very confident (blindfolded), **God is calling out to you. You can do what he asks you to do because you're sure he's there to help you.**

SCORE WITH SCRIPTURE

If you do not stand firm in your faith, you will not stand at all (Isaiah 7:9).

"SQUIRT THE SHIRT" JAMBOREE

No sitting around in this game! Kids will learn to step forward and take action as they strategize how to win this fun variation of base tag.

STARTING LINE

Dilute the paints. Fill the squirt bottles with diluted paints. Each team member needs a squirt bottle and a plain T-shirt. Make sure each team has a different color in their bottles.

Use yarn or streamers to mark off four squares, each three-feet by three-feet. Set the squares about 50 feet apart and form a diamond. Each team will have a "home base" and a "bean base" directly opposite. Put beanbags in each "bean base."

Assign each of the teams to their bases. **Your team is on a mission to get from your home base to your bean base.** Point to the bases. **When I blow the**

THE GET LIST

• spray bottles for each participant
• whistle
• large plain colored T-shirts
• large jars of washable tempera paints in two different colors
• beanbags
• yarn or streamers

Ages: 4th grade and up

Time: 15–30 minutes

Group size: large

Outdoor

Activity level: 3

Noise Meter: 3

Godprint:
Initiative

....

whistle, you'll have five minutes to get to your bean base and back again. But beware of a squirt on your shirt. As you cross the play area, try to squirt the other team's players. Home bases and bean bases are "free" areas where no one can squirt you. If you're feeling brave you can try to capture a beanbag for your team. Point to the beanbags in the bean base. **But you can only leave the bean base area with the beanbag if you have a clean shirt. And only one person from each team may be inside the bean base area. If someone squirts you while you're holding the beanbag, you have to return the beanbag to the bean base. The winning team is the first one to get all their players and a beanbag back to home base.**

If neither team wins a beanbag, give the teams some hints: throw the beanbags to clean-shirted players or surround a clean-shirted player for protection. Start another round. Continue until there are no clean-shirted people left or a team wins. Lift the clean-shirt rule if the kids are struggling. To play longer, have the teams switch spray bottles or turn the shirts inside out.

COACHING CHARACTER

- Why is it difficult to win this game?
- Was anything surprising about this game?
- Can you win this game without taking a risk?

Encourage kids to talk about the risks they had to take in order to play and win this game.

To help your team win this game, you had to step out and take action! If you stayed in a safe zone, you couldn't play. You would have missed out on all the action—and the fun! Ask a volunteer to read Galatians 6:9.

- How does this verse remind you of the game we just played? *(It says not to give up or become weary.)*
- What are some risks that you have to take in real life? What happens if you don't step out and take action?
- How does God help you step out and take action to do something good?

When you step out and take action in real life, the safety zone goes with you. That's because God is the safety zone. When you take the initiative to do something that God wants you to do, he'll give you the strength and courage to get the job done.

SCORE WITH SCRIPTURE

Let us not become weary in doing good, for at the proper time we will reap a harvest if we do not give up (Galatians 6:9).

STOMPING GOOD TIME

Stomping around on aluminum foil helps kids discover that friends working together can get the job done.

STARTING LINE

Before starting, tear off enough pieces of aluminum foil for each kid in your class to have one. The pieces should be large enough for the kids to step on and make a footprint. Have your kids sit in a large circle on the floor.

THE GET LIST
- aluminum foil

Let's get to know some different people in our group. I want each of you to figure out what your shoe size is. You may need to look inside your shoe or on the bottom of your shoe to find the size if you don't know. When I say "Shoe Fly!" shout out your shoe size and find someone else who has the same shoe size that you do. Keep shouting until you find someone. If no one has the same size as you, you may team up with someone who has almost the same size. When you've found a partner, sit down together.

Allow a few minutes for everyone to find someone to partner with, and then explain the next part of the game.

I'm going to give each of you a piece of aluminum foil and I want you to make an imprint of your partner's shoe with the foil. Then talk with your partner about how each shoe print is different or alike.

Kids who don't know their shoe size can pair up with someone about the same size. Allow a few minutes for the kids to accomplish this. Have them stand up and press one foot firmly into the aluminum foil. Then gather all the shoe prints. Scatter the prints around the perimeter of your room or area. **Now go with your partner and see if you can pick out your two prints from all the others. When you have the right ones, come back to the circle.**

COACHING CHARACTER

- What helped you find which shoe prints belonged to you and your partner? What made it difficult?
- Do you think it would have been easier or harder to find the right prints without your partner? Why?

God understands that we all need friends. It can be hard to find a good friend, just like it might have been hard to find the right shoe print. But the more we know about people, the more likely we are to find good friends, just as the more you knew about the shoe print the easier it was to find it. Ask a volunteer to read Ecclesiastes 4:9–10.

- According to this verse, why are two better than one?

Ages: K and up

Time: 15 minutes

Group size: large

Indoor/Outdoor

Activity level: 2

Noise Meter: 3

Godprint:
Friendliness

....

USE THIS GAME WITH:

- Ruth and Naomi, Ruth 1–4 (dedication in friendship).
- Jonathan and David, 1 Samuel 19, 20 (sacrificing for a friend).
- Elisha and Elijah, 2 Kings 2:1–13 (following a friend).

• Give me some examples of how friends help each other.

God created us to have a relationship with him and to have relationships with other people. Sometimes the friend God sends your way is just what you need!

SCORE WITH SCRIPTURE

Two are better than one, because they have a good return for their work: If one falls down, his friend can help him up (Ecclesiastes 4:9–10).

THE GREAT GARBAGE GAME

Ages: 4th grade and up

Time: 10 minutes

Group size: large

Indoor

Activity level: 3

Noise Meter: 3

Godprint:
Courage

....

USE THIS GAME WITH:

• David and the Giant, 1 Samuel 17:12–51 *(standing up against something scary, doing what you know is right even if you are afraid).*

• Daniel and the Lions, Daniel 6:1–28 *(trusting God to protect you in scary situations).*

Stand firm in the face of danger because God is with you! That's what kids will learn from being bombarded by newspaper wads with only a pie tin for protection.

THE GET LIST

• 8 large garbage bags
• aluminum pie tins
• newspaper
• treats in a box

STARTING LINE

Before the game begins have the kids wad up newspaper and tape the wads into balls the size of softballs. You'll need 40 balls altogether. Form two teams. Have the teams stand against the walls on opposite sides of the room. Give each team four garbage bags and 20 balls. Place the "prize box" in the middle of the room.

You're all on a mission to capture the prize box. Point to the box in the center of the room. **Each team will need to choose a king and queen.** Give them time to pick one of each. **Have your king and queen stand on a trash bag by your team's wall. Only a king or queen can capture the prize. Your team has to work together to help the king and queen move. Do this by putting the extra bag on the floor for the royals to step on. Then move the first bag for the next step. Keep moving the bags toward the center of the room. The king and queen cannot step on the floor.**

But wait! You're under attack! The rest of you are courageous warriors.

Warriors are in charge of two things: throwing garbage at the other team's king and queen and protecting their own king and queen with these. Give each player a pie tin. **Each team will try to dethrone the other team's king or queen by throwing garbage at them** (paper balls). **A king or queen hit by garbage must leave the bag and become a courageous warrior. Someone else becomes king or queen. But the new royal must start over by standing on a bag by the wall.**

Your team has to work together, protecting your king and queen, trying to advance them toward the prize box and dethroning the other team all at the same time.

Play until you have a winning team or your time is up.

COACHING CHARACTER

- What dangers did you face in this game?
- What protection did you have?
- Was the protection enough to keep you safe from danger? Why or why not?

Sometimes it seems that there is a lot of stuff in our lives trying to knock us off our course. It takes courage to do what we know is right. Let's find out where courage comes from. Ask a volunteer to read Psalm 23:4.

- What does this verse tell us is our protection against evil? *(God is with us.)*
- A rod and staff were tools a shepherd used to protect sheep. Why are they a comfort?

Newspaper wads can't really hurt us, and pie tins are not much protection against something that could hurt us. But the game helps us think about God's protection. We all get frightened by some things. Courage doesn't mean you're never scared. Courage means that we can stand firm when we're in danger because God is with us and gives us his strength.

SCORE WITH SCRIPTURE

Even though I walk through the valley of the shadow of death, I will fear no evil; for you are with me; your rod and your staff, they comfort me (Psalm 23:4).

GET, GET, GIVE!

Kids will find themselves in a tough spot–and learn they can be unselfish and encourage others.

STARTING LINE

Hand out the slips of paper to the kids. Have them write their names on the papers and then collect them in an empty tissue box. Then have the kids remove their shoes and sit in a large circle. Place the box of names in the center of the circle. Stand in the center of the circle.

This is the Gush Pot, a place of honor! I'll choose our first Giver. Draw a name from the box. Model how to say something complimentary about that person, and then hand the person the two empty tissue boxes. **These aren't ordinary boxes. They're scooters! Put one on each foot and scoot around the circle. As you go, gently tap everyone's head, saying, "Get," until you're ready to choose a person by calling out "Give." Call out the person's name. Then try to scoot around the circle and sit in that person's spot. The other player will try to catch you. If you're caught, go to the box and draw a name and give encouragement to the person whose name is on the paper. Then that person becomes the next "scooter."** If you make it back to the empty spot, the other person becomes the new scooter.

THE GET LIST

- at least 3 full size empty tissue boxes
- slips of paper
- pencils or pens

Ages: K–3rd grade

Time: 20 minutes

Group size: large

Indoor

Activity level: 3

Noise Meter: 2

Godprint:
Unselfishness

USE THIS GAME WITH:

- The poor widow, Mark 12:41–44 *(give without expecting reward).*

- The Good Samaritan, Luke 10:25–37 *(be unselfish with everyone).*

- Paul is shipwrecked, Acts 27:1–28:10 *(encourage others unselfishly).*

Play for several rounds.

COACHING CHARACTER

- Why was it an honor to be in the Gush Pot?
- Do you think it's harder to give or receive a compliment or word of encouragement?
- What are some other ways we can give unselfishly to others?

God wants us to be unselfish. Who is the best example of unselfishness we can think of? *(Jesus.)* **He gave his life for us even though he didn't deserve to die.** Ask a volunteer to read Acts 20:35.

When you feel caught, or find yourself in a tough spot, you can still unselfishly think of others and give encouragement. You'll be amazed at how the blessings come back to encourage you!

SCORE WITH SCRIPTURE

In everything I did, I showed you that by this kind of hard work we must help the weak, remembering the words the Lord Jesus himself said: "It is more blessed to give than to receive" (Acts 20:35).

PASS THE CUBE

Have an arctic blast as kids use cool-ordination and cool-operation to pass an ice cube to other team members.

Ages: K and up

Time: 10–15 minutes

Group size: 6 or more

Indoor/Outdoor

Activity level: 3

Noise Meter: 3

Godprint:
Cooperation

....

THE GET LIST

- buckets
- ice cubes
- tongs
- spatulas
- spoons
- ladles

STARTING LINE

Prepare or gather ice cubes, all the same size (bigger is better). Assign kids into teams of three or four players. Each team will need two buckets and a set of kitchen utensils. Set a bucket of ice for each team at one end of the room and place an empty bucket about 20–40 feet away. Have each team spread out its players from one bucket to the other.

This game will take some cool-ordination and cool-operation. Hand each team player a kitchen utensil. **This is your cool-tool. The first person will use a cool-tool to take an ice cube from the bucket. He or she will use the tool to carry it to the next player on the team. You'll pass the ice cube from player to player with the cool-tools. The last person will put the ice cube in the empty bucket. The ice cube must be transported by the cool-tool. If the ice cube falls off the cool-tool, or if anything other than the cool-tools touch the ice cube, like hot little fingers, then that ice cube will not count. You'll have three minutes to get as many ice cubes into the bucket as possible. The team with the most ice cubes in the empty bucket wins.**

If you play more than once you might wish to switch the order of the cool-tools and the players.

COACHING CHARACTER

• How well did your team work together?
• How well do you think you would have done if you had to do all the parts of the game by yourself?

It's important to do some things for ourselves like reading and riding a bike. But we can't do everything alone. Cool-operating and helping each other can make things easier for all of us and is pretty cool. Have a volunteer read Ephesians 4:16.

• What does this verse teach us about cooperation? *(Everyone has a part to do.)*
• When we do God's work, what holds us all together? *(God himself.)*

We're a part of a big team, God's team. We each have talents to help God's team out. When we use our abilities to work toward the same goal, we accomplish more and that is way cool.

SCORE WITH SCRIPTURE

From him the whole body, joined and held together by every supporting ligament, grows and builds itself up in love, as each part does its work (Ephesians 4:16).

USE THIS GAME WITH:

• Moses and Aaron, Exodus 6:28–19:25 *(work together to lead the people).*

• Ezra and Nehemiah, Nehemiah 6–8 *(work together to rebuild Jerusalem and bring the people back).*

SPLASH AND DASH

While sloshing around the field, kids will discover that staying full of the "living water" and turning the right direction help to reach the goal faster.

STARTING LINE

Assign the group to two equal teams. Split the field in half and place a different colored bucket at each end of the field. Mark off a masking tape end zone for each team. Fill the two other buckets with water and set one on each sideline. Each team needs to select a bucket catcher. Send this player to the opposite side of the field to the bucket.

Each team will be trying to score in its team's bucket. The catcher may hold the bucket to try and catch sponges but cannot move from his or her spot.

Get ready to throw some sponges! Each team will try to throw sponges into its team bucket. Make sure each team knows which bucket they are trying to score in.

THE GET LIST

• four large sponges
• four buckets; two must be different colors
• masking tape

Ages: 3rd grade and up

Time: 15 minutes

Group size: large

Outdoor

Activity level: 3

Noise Meter: 3

Godprint: *Repentance*

USE THIS GAME WITH:

- David confesses his sins, 2 Samuel 12:1–20 (*David turns towards God*).

- Jonah goes to Nineveh, Jonah 1–4 (*going in the wrong direction and turning around*).

- Saul becomes Paul Acts 22:1–17 (*a turn towards God*).

Now here's the tricky part. To dash around the room you must not have a sponge. If you have a sponge in your hand you cannot move. To pass a sponge to another teammate, you must turn around and toss it backwards. To score the sponge in the bucket you may turn towards the bucket and try to toss it in. The bucket goalie cannot move but can hold the bucket and try to catch the sponges you toss.

Use the buckets of water on the sidelines to refill the sponge. You might find that a sponge throws better when it is heavy with water. The team with the most sponges in the bucket wins.

Start the teams on the opposite side of the room from their bucket and goalie. Toss the dry sponges out to two players on each team. Decide how long you will play, then call time or end the game when one team has all the sponges.

COACHING CHARACTER

- Was it easier to toss the sponge to a teammate or towards the bucket? Why?
- How much trouble did you have remembering which way you should be facing?

In the game we just played, it was hard to see what you were doing when you had your backs turned toward your teammates. You couldn't see where to toss the sponge or even where the goal—the bucket—was. When you turned and faced the goal, then it was easier. Ask a volunteer to read Hebrews 12:1 and the first part of verse 2.

- Tell me something about this verse that reminds you of the game.
- What things keep us from seeing our goal to reach God?
- What kinds of choices do we make every day that are like turning our backs on God?

Sin keeps us from seeing where God wants us to run. But when we repent and turn around, we can run the race he wants us to run. When we keep our eyes focused and turned towards God we will score a goal in the bucket of our lives.

SCORE WITH SCRIPTURE

Therefore, since we are surrounded by such a great cloud of witnesses, let us throw off everything that hinders and the sin that so easily entangles, and let us run with perseverance the race marked out for us (Hebrews 12:1).

LEMON FRESH!

This refreshing game will make kids pucker up with enthusiasm as they creatively come up with a cheer to keep them lemon fresh.

STARTING LINE

On each card write one of the following words or phrases; Hip-hip hooray; hallelujah; twist and shout; jumping for joy; get all excited; yippee-skippy; and boogie-woogie. Keep the cards in a pile facing down. Write the numbers one through four spaced out on the lemon.

Have the kids form small teams. Hand each team a lemon. **When is the last time you ate a lemon?** Take several responses. **Wow, are those things sour! Just about everyone cringed when I mentioned eating a lemon. Now can you think of ways to use lemons that put a smile on people's faces?** (In their drinks, lemon pie, lemon fresh scent of detergent and good smelling things.) **Lemons can be used to refresh, rejuvenate and add a splash of sunlight to anyone's stinky day.**

Let's show God a lemon fresh attitude. As a team you'll roll this lemon to find out how many cards your team gets to draw from the pile. Hold up the lemon with the numbers on it. Point to the pile of index cards. **Your team will then use the words drawn from the pile to make up a cheer that can change your attitude from sour to a splash of refreshing joy. Your team must use the lemon in some way during the cheer. I'll give you a few minutes to get your terrific cheers together. Then you can show all of us your splashing and enthusiastic cheers for God.**

COACHING CHARACTER

- When you show a sour attitude towards things, what does this tell others about you? What does it tell others about your love for God?
- What's the opposite of a sour lemon attitude?

Sometimes it can be hard to keep from getting a sour attitude about work, school, home and even church. What do you think would happen if we could wipe those sour attitudes away and replace them with a splash of refreshing enthusiasm? Ask a volunteer to read Psalm 98:1.

- According to this verse, why should we sing to the Lord?
- How is a "new song" like a "new attitude?"

When you feel those stinky feelings creeping in just use your cheer to wipe them away. Sing a new song to show your lemon fresh attitude.

SCORE WITH SCRIPTURE

Sing to the Lord a new song, for he has done marvelous things (Psalm 98:1).

THE GET LIST

- lemons
- permanent marker
- index cards

Ages: 1st grade and up

Time: 20 minutes

Group size: medium

Indoor

Activity level: 3

Noise Meter: 3

Godprint:
Enthusiasm

. . . .

USE THIS GAME WITH:

- Song of praise, Psalm 100 *(shout for joy to the Lord).*

- John the Baptist, Mark 1:1–8 *(An enthusiastic attitude about God's work).*

SMASH AND DASH

Ages: K–2nd grade

Time: 20 minutes

Group size: medium to large

Outdoor

Activity level: 3

Noise Meter: 3

Godprint:
Worship

. . . .

USE THIS GAME WITH:

• Birth of Jesus, Luke 2:1–20 *(worship the Savior).*

• Palm Sunday, Luke 19:29–38 *(the people praise Jesus as king).*

Have a smashing, dashing time as kids learn about worshiping God. God is worthy of our praise, attention and honor.

THE GET LIST

• jars of bubble mixture

STARTING LINE

Form equal teams for a relay race. Have each team form a line. **God deserves a smashing round of thanks for being the wonderful, loving Creator he is! Let's think of some ways that we can thank him. During this game you're going to give a little worship clap and shout. Let's think of a worship phrase that we can shout during our game.** The kids can make up their own praises or you can teach them a phrase to repeat as they clap out each word. Here are some examples to teach the kids.

• Thank you Jesus for…(let them fill in the blank.)
• Praise God for all things above and below.
• God is awesome!
• Great is the Lord and worthy of praise.

Give the second person in each line a jar of bubble mixture. **When I say "Smash and dash," each team will begin. The person with the bubbles will dip the wand into the bubble mixture and gently blow some bubbles. The first person in line must smash all of the bubbles by giving great big claps. With each clap must shout out words of praise or thanks.**

When you've smashed all the bubbles, the first person in line dashes to the end of the room (show them where they must dash to) **and sits at the back of the line. The person who was holding the bubbles hands the jar to the next person. The "blower" becomes the "smash and dasher." Let's see which team can be the first to have all their members dash to the end of the room.**

Make sure you ask if anyone has any questions. **Is everyone ready to give God a great big cheer! Ready set, "smash and dash."**

COACHING CHARACTER

Gather the kids and collect the bubble mixture. Have a volunteer read Psalm 145:3.

• What is so great about God?
• How often do you think about how great God is?

Worshiping God is telling him how much you love him. There are all kinds of ways to show God that you love him. Some people worship God quietly and some people worship God loudly.

• How can you show God that you love him?
• What's your favorite way to worship God?

We worship in ways that express the feelings of our hearts. Right now I'm feeling something really big! Let's give God a great big cheer. Repeat after me: Thank you, God, for all you do! Thank you, God; we love you too!

SCORE WITH SCRIPTURE

*Great is the L*ORD *and most worthy of praise; His greatness no-one can fathom (Psalm 145:3).*

Kids will learn the importance of recognizing right from wrong as they create and play with paper airplanes with an attitude.

STARTING LINE

Use masking tape to make a large circle on the floor. **Have you ever heard of flying fish? Well, get ready, because you're about to make some—then capture them!** Give each player a sheet of paper. **Use this paper to create a flying fish. Start out like a paper airplane, then draw features or add special folds to make it "fishy."**

When kids have finished their fish, gather everyone around the masking tape circle. **Everyone join me here at our "pond." Let's see—I'm looking for a great pair of fish lips. Everyone, show me your best fish lips.** Have the kids make fish lips and choose the person with the best fish lips to go first.

All right, I'll need (Mr. or Ms.) **Fish Lips in the center of the pond, please. Now we need to cover up those eyes.** Blindfold the player. Then give him or her the fishnet. **Can you feel what I've put in your hands? When I give the signal, the fish are going to fly across the circle and you're going to use the net to catch as many fish as you can.**

Step outside the circle. **When I say, "Fly those fish!" everyone around the circle will fly their fish to someone across the circle. Mr.** (or Mrs.) **Fish Lips will swing the net and catch as many as possible. If a fish lands in the circle and is not caught in the net, anyone can pick it up, return to the edge of the circle and fly it again. Keep flying the fish until I shout out, "Frozen fish!"**

Start the game. Call out "frozen fish" after thirty seconds. Allow the player with the net to remove the blindfold, then resume play for another thirty seconds. Let the person in the middle choose the next player to stand in the middle. Give each "netter" an opportunity to "fish" both with and without the blindfold.

COACHING CHARACTER

Let kids retrieve their own flying fish, then gather everyone in a circle on the floor. To avoid distraction, have kids place the fish behind them.

THE GET LIST

- fishnet
- copy paper
- blindfold
- scissors
- markers
- masking tape

Ages: 3rd grade and up

Time: 25 minutes

Group size: 10–15

Indoor (high ceiling)

Activity level: 2

Noise Meter: 2

Godprint:
Discipleship

. . . .

USE THIS GAME WITH:

- Conversion of Saul, Acts 9 (Paul literally becomes blind, then God opens his eyes).

- Paul and the Philippian jailer, Acts 16:16–24 (Paul witnesses to the jailer).

- What was it like trying to net the flying fish when you couldn't see them?
- What are some of the things life "throws at you" that are hard to handle?

Have a volunteer read Psalm 119:18. **We never know what life is going to throw at us—sickness, a tough time at school, family squabbles. Sometimes it feels like we're blindfolded and it's all we can do to handle the things that come our way.**

But God's Word takes the blinders off. It helps us understand that God is in control and that we have lots of wonderful people standing beside us. You know, some people have never had their eyes opened to the great things in God's Word. They don't know about God's love and forgiveness and help. So we have a job to do! Don't let the people you know go through life with blinders on. Open their eyes to God's goodness. Spread the good news of God's love!

SCORE WITH SCRIPTURE

Open my eyes that I may see wonderful things in your law (Psalm 119:18).

PULL MY STRING

Ages: 4th grade and up

Time: 30 minutes

Group size: any

Indoor

Activity level: 2

Noise Meter: 2

Godprint:
Community

. . . .

USE THIS GAME WITH:

• The early church, Acts 4:34–37 *(working and sharing together)*.

• Priscilla and Aquila Acts 18:2–3, 26 *(working together to build the body of Christ)*.

Watch the fun and laughter as kids work together to create a puppet and learn that the church community works together as a body.

THE GET LIST

• newspaper
• string
• masking tape
• index cards
• markers
• whiteboard

STARTING LINE

Use the tape to mark start and stop lines about 10 to 12 feet apart. Form teams of four. Provide each team with all the materials and five index cards. On a board write the Bible verse, dividing it into five chunks.

• Now you are the
• body of Christ
• and each one of you
• is a part of it.
• 1 Corinthians 12:27

Let's see if we can all walk away today with a new Bible verse. Let's start by making a puppet. Wad up the newspaper and use the tape to make a head, a body, two arms and two legs. Pause to give kids time to do this much. **Tie long strings to each arm and leg to make the puppet. On each of the index cards write one of the segments to the Bible verse. Tape the cards to the arms, legs and head.**

Now we're going to walk away with a new Bible verse. Each team member is in charge of one of the strings and the attached Bible verse segment. As a team you'll walk your puppet across the floor to the end of the tapeline. Start by saying the reference on your puppet all together. Then the person in charge of the string attached to the next segment of the verse says that part and moves forward one step. The rest of the team members do the same in the order of the Bible verse. Keep repeating the order until you've reached the finish line. And don't forget to say the reference as a team before repeating the beginning of the Bible verse.

When all the teams reach the finish line, ask each team to recite the complete verse by presenting a puppet show with its character.

COACHING CHARACTER

• What decisions did you have to make to work together making the puppet?
• What would have happened if only one person on your team moved a puppet body part?

Read aloud 1 Corinthians 12:12–27.

• How do the people in a church community work together?
The church is the body of Christ and we need each other. We each have different

things to do to help. If the church were a puppet, we'd all have a different string to tug. The body doesn't work right when one part isn't helping. God wants us to work together to help each other cross the finish line.

SCORE WITH SCRIPTURE

Now you are the body of Christ and each one of you is a part of it (1 Corinthians 12:27).

Roll 'em, roll 'em, roll 'em, keep those verses rollin'. This game gives kids the opportunity to roll out a Bible verse with enthusiasm about God's Word.

STARTING LINE

Before class write a word from the Bible verse on each paper towel sheet: "Whatever you do, whether in word or deed, do it all in the name of the Lord Jesus, giving thanks to God (Colossians 3:17)." Jumble up the order, and don't tear off the paper towel sheets. Keep them attached to the paper towel roll. To make things more difficult, depending on the abilities of your group, eliminate capital letters and punctuation. You can also use only one letter per towel, color coding the words so the kids can find the letters that go together. Circle a letter if it is the beginning of a word as an extra clue. Prepare one rolled-up verse for each group of four or five.

Group kids into teams of four or five. Each team will need a marked roll of paper towels, two empty paper towel tubes, and a bunch of clear tape.

As a team your mission is to unroll the paper towels. Carefully tear each sheet apart. Put the sheets in order to form the Bible verse. Then tape the sheets together in the right order. Attach the first sheet and last sheet to a paper towel tube. This will make a scroll.

Here's the challenge: the team that gets the job done with the most enthusiasm wins. Let's hear some cheering and words of encouragement for each other as you play. Encourage kids to practice some quick cheers for each other. Hand one person on each team a piece of paper and a pencil. **The "enthusiasm keeper" will make a mark on the paper each time he or she hears someone on your team saying something enthusiastic about the job you're doing together. I'll also time you to see which team is fastest—but don't forget to be enthusiastic.** When teams are finished, find out how many marks the "enthusiasm keepers" made. If you like, you can reward both the most enthusiastic and the fastest group.

THE GET LIST

- full paper towel rolls
- empty paper towel tubes
- clear tape
- marker
- stopwatch or clock with second hand
- paper and pencil

Ages: 2nd grade and up

Time: 10–15 minutes

Group size: large

Indoor

Activity level: 2

Noise Meter: 2

Godprint: *Enthusiasm*

USE THIS GAME WITH:

- Tabitha, Acts 9:36–42 *(joyful servants make an impact on other).*
- Paul and Silas in prison, Acts 16:25–34 *(rejoicing in trials leads others to Christ).*

COACHING CHARACTER

• What did you think when you saw all those jumbled words and letters?
• How did you feel about hearing others in your group cheer each other on?
• What's more important, being fast, or being enthusiastic? Why? *(Kids will have opinions on both sides. It's important to get the job done, but God wants us to be enthusiastic as well.)*

Repeat Colossians 3:17 together.

• What attitude should we have about everything we do?
• What might make it hard for you to be enthusiastic sometimes?
• How does enthusiasm catch on?

God wants us to have a glad spirit about the work that he gives us to do. Some people find it easy to be enthusiastic for Jesus. For others, it's harder. But when we do what God wants us to do, we can be sure we're doing the right thing—and that's a good reason to be glad about doing it.

SCORE WITH SCRIPTURE

Whatever you do, whether in word or deed, do it all in the name of the Lord Jesus, giving thanks to God (Colossians 3:17).

UNDERCOVER VERSE

Ages: 2nd grade and up

Time: 30 minutes

Group size: 4 or more

Indoor

Activity level: 1

Noise Meter: 1

Godprint:
Cooperation

It's time to solve a mystery with the help of your classroom spies. In this memory game, kids learn the contents and sequence of a Scripture verse. They'll work together to keep from getting confused with a few wrong words.

THE GET LIST

• 30 paper plates
• markers
• clothesline
• clothespins
• markers

STARTING LINE

You'll need 19 different paper plates to write each word and the reference to Romans 12:5: "So in Christ we who are many form one body, and each member belongs to all the others." Write one of the following words on the remaining paper plates: on, few, between, Jesus, two, over, let, but, they, make and some. Arrange the plates upside down on the floor, in a 5-plate by 6-plate rectangle. Hang the clothesline in the room at a height kids can reach. Have the clothespins handy to display the paper plates as kids find them.

I need all my undercover agents to join me over here by our super duper spy board. Gather the kids around the grid. **You're all undercover spies and your mission is to uncover our Bible verse. We'll take turns flipping over these mystery plates. We're looking for the words and the reference to our memory verse. Here's the sneaky part. If you turn over a plate and it has a word from the verse on it, it must be in the correct**

order of the verse. If it is in the correct order you get to hang it on the spy line. Point to the clothesline. **If the plate has a word that's not in the verse or a word that's not the next word in the verse, turn the plate back over in the same spot. Then the next spy gets a turn. But remember what you saw so you'll be ready when we need it. With everybody's cooperation, we should be able to uncover the entire Bible verse! Is everyone ready?** Choose the person whose name starts closest to the letter "S" for spy. Then have the rest of the kids take turns in a counter-clockwise direction. Kids who uncover the right word can hang it on the clothesline.

COACHING CHARACTER

• Would this game be easier or harder to play by yourself? Why do you think so?
• What kinds of things can people do to make the game easier?

You all did your part to uncover the Bible verse. What one person forgot, someone else remembered. If you had to depend on just your own memory, you might have had a really tough time.

Let's read the verse together. Lead the kids in reading the verse aloud together from the clothesline and show your Bible open to Romans 12:5.

• Who is most important in the body of Christ? *(Everyone!)*
• How can "many" form one body?
• How did we work together as one body in the memory game?

God's plan is for everyone in his body—the church—to work together. Each of us has special gifts from God. While we're very good at some things, we might need lots of help to do other things. That's when we need each other most! When we all use our gifts and cooperate with one another, we can do great things for Jesus.

SCORE WITH SCRIPTURE

So in Christ we who are many form one body, and each member belongs to all the others (Romans 12:5).

USE THIS GAME WITH:

• Abraham and Lot dividing the land, Genesis 13:1–12 *(cooperating together for a peaceable solution).*

• Rebuilding the walls of Jerusalem, Nehemiah 2:11–6:15 *(working together with a common goal).*

• Four friends bring a paralyzed man to Jesus, Mark 2:1–12 *(working together to minister to someone else).*

CHALK ONE UP FOR GOD

Ages: 3rd grade and up

Time: 10 minutes

Group size: small to medium

Indoor

Activity level: 2

Noise Meter: 3

Godprint:
Worship

....

USE THIS GAME WITH:

• Worship Christ the king, Matthew 2:2 *(an example of how others came to worship the king).*

• Let us kneel down before the Lord, Psalm 95:6 *(experience another form of worship— kneeling).*

Offering praises to God and learning Bible verses with a twist is the focus of this fun and cooperative relay-style game. Kids encounter the Bible verse over and over while working together to complete a task.

THE GET LIST

• two pieces of chalk
• two cone-shaped party hats
• two small chalkboards
• Bible
• two bowls or containers
• index cards

STARTING LINE

Place two small chalkboards at one end of the room. Write the Bible verse on index cards, one word on each card, including the reference: "You are my God and I will give you thanks; you are my God, I will exalt you (Psalm 118:28)." Make two sets. Place each set of Bible verse cards in a bowl or container. Use the masking tape to make a start line as far away as possible from the chalkboards. Set the containers, a piece of chalk and a hat by each start line. Then count off and form two teams. Ask kids to sit in a line on the masking tape and face the end of the room with the chalkboards.

Give the first player on each team the party hat and a piece of chalk. **When I shout "Hallelujah," the first player on each team picks out a card from the container. Tuck it inside the party hat and put the hat on your forehead. Then use the tip of the hat to push the chalk along the floor all the way to the chalkboard. When you get to the chalkboard, take your card out and write the word on the chalkboard. Leave the card in front of the chalkboard. Then run back to your team and hand the hat and chalk to the next player. The next player will then draw a card, tuck the card in the hat and roll the chalk toward the board. Once you've drawn all the cards out of the bowl, work together with your team to unscramble the cards and put the Bible verse in order. Then write the verse on the board in the right order. Once you think you have the verse written correctly, shout out, "Praise the Lord!"**

If kids are struggling to get the words in the proper order, provide a Bible for them to refer to. Once kids have written the verse correctly on both boards, have the teams recite the verse together. Have everyone shout, "Praise the Lord" together.

COACHING CHARACTER

When both teams have a complete verse, gather the kids and read the verse together aloud from the chalkboard.

• Tell me the main words of this verse. *(God, thanks, exalt.)*
• What's the hardest word for you to understand? *(Kids will probably choose "exalt." It means "give glory or praise.")*

When we played this game, we saw one word of the verse at a time, until we had

all the words on the board. Then we had the big picture of worshiping God. When we worship God, we put this verse into action. We show God that we believe he deserves the best praise we can offer.

People can worship God in so many different ways—quietly, loudly, sitting still or moving around. Worship God your way. Tell him how thankful you are that he is your God.

SCORE WITH SCRIPTURE
You are my God and I will give you thanks; you are my God, and I will exalt you (Psalm 118:28).

UNTANGLE SELFISHNESS

The kids will twist and weave and giggle as they learn to work together unselfishly to untangle the memory verse.

STARTING LINE
Cut ribbons into strips three feet long. Write parts of the memory verse on four different colored ribbons. For example, on the red ribbon write, "Do nothing out of selfish ambition." On the blue ribbon write, "or vain conceit." On the green ribbon write, "but in humility consider." On the white ribbon write, "others better than yourselves." A red, blue, green and white ribbon with the parts of the verse makes one set of ribbons. Make sure that each set of ribbons has four colors and a complete memory verse when put together. Tangle and twist each set of four ribbons, but do not tie knots.

Assign the group into teams of four. You'll need a set of ribbons for each team. Have each group sit in a circle facing each other. Place the tangled set of ribbons in the center of each circle.

Okey-dokey, everyone, let's do the hokey pokey! Put your right hand in and grab the end of a ribbon. Now do the hokey pokey again and reach in with your left hand and grab the end of a different colored ribbon. Look at your hands. Are you hanging onto two different colored ribbons? If not, have the group let go of the ribbons and try again. **Great! When I say. "Untangle!" try to untangle the ribbons. Here's the tricky part; you cannot let go of your ribbons. You might have to do crazy moves going over and under each other's arms. But with a lot of kindness and unselfishness toward each other as you tug and pull at the ribbons, eventually you'll untangle the mess.**

Once the ribbons are freed, have the team tie the ribbons together to form the Bible verse

COACHING CHARACTER
• While you were untangling, did you want to go first? How hard was it to be patient and take turns?
• How did you feel when someone else made a good move and helped with the untangling?

THE GET LIST
• red, blue, green and white wide ribbon
• markers

Ages: 3rd grade and up

Time: 15–20 minutes

Group size: small to large

Indoor/Outdoor

Activity level: 3

Noise Meter: 3

Godprint:
Unselfishness

. . . .

USE THIS GAME WITH:
• Rebecca shares water, Genesis 24:15–20 *(going beyond the call of duty).*

• A boy shares his lunch, John 6:8–11 *(thinking of others before yourself).*

At the beginning of our game, the ribbons were in knots. You may have thought that you could untangle the knot all by yourself. Maybe you thought you could do it faster, or you just felt like doing it yourself. Instead, the rules of the game said you had to work with the other players. So you couldn't do just what you wanted to do. Let's say the verse together one more time. Repeat Philippians 2:3.

• How does this verse remind you of the game?
• Describe some times when it's hard for you to do what someone else would like to do.
• Tell me how you feel when you think about someone else before you think about what you want.

Sometimes our lives are in knots. We get all tied up in knots about something that happens at school or at home, or with a friend. You never know when you might be the person that God uses to help untie someone else's knot. When we think of others before we think of ourselves, God uses us to help other people.

SCORE WITH SCRIPTURE

Do nothing out of selfish ambition or vain conceit, but in humility consider others better than yourselves (Philippians 2:3).

COUNTING CLUES

Ages: 3rd grade and up

Time: 10 minutes

Group size: small to medium

Indoor

Activity level: 1

Noise Meter: 1

Godprint:
Honesty

What can kids learn by playing with cereal pieces on a table? They can learn Bible verses about honesty–and practice being honest at the same time.

THE GET LIST

• cereal
• paper
• pens
• sandwich bags
• index cards

STARTING LINE

Put a handful of cereal into a sandwich bag for each pair of kids. On each index card write the Bible verse: "The Lord detests lying lips, but he delights in men who are truthful" (Proverbs 12:22). You'll need one card for each pair.

Everyone will need a partner. Hand out a piece of paper, a pen and a bag of cereal to each pair. **One of you needs to be the Clue Giver and the other the Chomper.** Pause and let kids decide their roles. **I'm going to hand the Clue Givers a clue card; keep it a secret from the Chomper.** Hand the Clue Givers the index card with the Bible verse on it. **Clue Givers, on the piece of paper in front of you, write down a blank space for each word on the card.** You may need to tell kids how many blanks to put on the paper. For example, for the Bible verse Proverbs 12:22, they'll need to make 14 blanks, which includes one for the reference. **Chompers, count the blanks on the paper and set out the same number of pieces of cereal.**

Now the fun part! The Chomper tries to guess the words to the Bible verse that belong in the blanks. Here are the rules. The Clue Giver gives one word at a time as a clue. But don't use any of the words from the actual Bible verse.

If the Chomper guesses correctly, the Clue Giver writes the word in the appropriate space on the paper. If the guess is wrong, the Chomper must eat one of the pieces

of cereal. **If the Chomper eats all the cereal before guessing the verse, your team is finished. If your team finishes the Bible verse and you have cereal left over, we'll count the remaining cereal pieces. The pair with the most remaining cereal wins the round.**

Play multiple rounds using different Bible verses. Have the partners on the teams switch roles.

COACHING CHARACTER
- Clue Givers, were you tempted to give clues that would be extra tricky? What did you do?
- Chompers, how did you feel about playing this game without looking over at another pair's paper? Explain.

Repeat Proverbs 12:22 together.

- What does God think about truthfulness?
- Why is honesty important to God?

God wants you to tell the truth in all that you do. Sometimes that's easy, like in this game. Other times it's not so easy.

- What makes it hard to be truthful?
- Can you lie without saying anything? Explain.
- What can help you be more truthful with others?

God is truthful. He doesn't lie or try to trick us. When we're honest, we show what God is like to other people, and he takes extra delight in the way that we serve him.

SCORE WITH SCRIPTURE
The Lord detests lying lips, but he delights in men who are truthful (Proverbs 12:22).

USE THIS GAME WITH:
- Samuel speaks honestly to his people, 1 Samuel 12:1–5 *(being honest with other people).*
- Zacchaeus admits to cheating people, Luke 19:1–10 *(how to make good for dishonest dealings).*

S.W.A.T. (SCORE WITH A TAP)

Buzz, buzz, buzz—kids can learn a favorite Bible verse with a SWAT. Watch them keep up with the fly swatter and buzz their way into the Bible.

STARTING LINE
Print the memory verse on the chalkboard, widely spaced, including the reference: "Let the Lord make you strong. Depend on his mighty power (Ephesians 6:10)."

Buzzzz. What's that noise? Do you hear that buzz? Get all the kids buzzing with you. **Buzzz.** Bring out the fly swatter. **Let's swat that buzz! You keep buzzing. But when you see me swat one of the Bible verse words on the board, call out that word. Ready?**

THE GET LIST
- fly swatter
- chalkboard
- chalk (or dry erase materials)

Ages: 2nd grade and up

Time: 15 minutes

Group size: any

Indoor

Activity level: 1

Noise Meter: 2

Godprint:
Perseverance

- Paul's thorn in the flesh, 2 Corinthians 12:1–10 (*Paul keeps going even when he feels weak*).

- Persistent widow, Luke 18:1–8 (*doesn't give up asking*).

Keep the kids buzzing and swat at the first word of the verse. Make sure they call it out. Keep buzzing. Go all the way through the verse. Then go through the verse one or two more times, a little bit faster.

Once you think the kids know the verse fairly well, have them stand up and form a line. **Now it's your turn to swat!** Hand the fly swatter to the first person in line. **We'll buzz again. When it's your turn, you choose when we should say the next word of the verse. Take the fly swatter, swat a word, then pass the fly swatter on to the next person in line.**

Go through the line a couple of times, making sure everyone has a turn. **Now let's speed things up. This time we don't want to hear any flies buzzing at all! But we don't want any empty spaces, either. Let's swat the words and hand off the fly swatter as quickly as we can to keep the verse going smoothly.**

Play as many rounds as you'd like to make sure the kids have learned the verse.

COACHING CHARACTER

- Tell me how our game got harder and harder as we went along.
- How many of you felt like quitting at some point?
- Why do people give up and quit when things get tough?

When things start to get tough or you're feeling hurt or worn out, you might think it's easier to "just quit." Some of you might have looked at this Bible verse and just wanted to quit before you even got started. But you kept on going and some of you surprised yourself with your ability to memorize the Bible verse.

- What can you learn from this verse to help you the next time you feel like giving up?

God wants us always to work hard and do our best. God is always there for us, cheering us on, especially when things are tough. God can make you strong.

SCORE WITH SCRIPTURE

Be strong in the Lord and in his mighty power (Ephesians 6:10).

POWER PUFF PRAISE

Ages: 3rd grade and up

Time: 10 minutes

Group size: 8–10

Outdoor

Activity level: 3

Noise Meter: 3

Godprint:
Worship

Whether in video games or movies, the character with the most power ultimately wins the game—and the glory. Trust is also a powerful thing. Relying on God completely helps "win the game."

THE GET LIST

- yarn
- cardboard
- scissors
- wrapped treats

STARTING LINE

Before game time, have kids make a Power Puff from the yarn. Wrap a healthy mound of yarn around a 2-inch piece of cardboard. Thread a small piece of yarn under the mound and tie it off in the middle. Slip the yarn from the cardboard and then cut the end loops apart. Fluff out each Power Puff. Separate your class or group into two teams

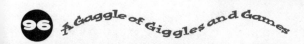

at one end of the playing area. Spread out treats at the other end. **Our Bible verse for today says, "Lord, you are great and powerful. Glory, majesty and beauty belong to you (1 Chronicles 29:11)."** Ask kids to repeat the verse, including the reference. Then have them hold up their Power Puffs. **What things of beauty! Power Puffs unite!**

Point to the treats. **See all the treats out yonder? To get one you must be a trustworthy team player. Team members: line up side-by-side. Place your Power Puff behind your knee, squat down, join arms with your teammates and try to jump towards the treats all while shouting 1 Chronicles 29:11!** You may want to have your kids practice jumping together. **This will take lots of leg and lung power. But I trust you can do it! If a Power Puff or a team member falls to the ground, or if no one on the team knows the next part of the verse, the team must start back at the starting line. The team to stay in line, get to the treats, all while shouting today's verse will be known as—are you ready?—the most worshipful kids on the planet!**

COACHING CHARACTER

• What was the hardest part of the verse to learn?
• How did you feel when you could say the whole thing?
• On a scale of 1 to 10, how much better was the verse when everyone on the team could say it?

Your whole team came together for one big effort of praise! And you had to pay attention to do this. You had to concentrate on the words of the verse and pay attention to where your power puff was and what the other people on your team were doing. As you learned the verse, the praise got bigger and bigger! God deserves the highest honor we can give him. He's worthy of our best attention.

SCORE WITH SCRIPTURE

Yours, O Lord, is the greatntess and the power and the glory and the majesty and the splendor, for everything in heaven and earth is yours (1 Chronicles 29:11).

USE THIS GAME WITH:

• Solomon builds the temple, 1 Kings 8 *(Solomon leads the people in worship).*

• Hezekiah cleans the temple, 2 Chronicles 29 *(the people worship together in the temple).*

SQUARE OFF

Ages: K and up

Time: 5 minutes

Group size: small to medium

Indoor

Activity level: 2

Noise Meter: 2

Godprint:
Generosity

....

USE THIS GAME WITH:

Use this game with any Bible verse. Just adjust the number of squares in the winning envelope.

How do you get kids to love memorizing God's Word? Don't let them know it's work! Keeping kids involved and active is the key to turning work into play. This simple game helps kids memorize verses while giving a little to each other.

THE GET LIST
- paper cups
- colored envelopes
- construction paper
- slips of paper
- basket

STARTING LINE

Cut from construction paper lots of 1" x 1" squares. Use the Bible verse, "A friend loves at all times" (Proverbs 17:17). This verse has eight words including the reference. Tape eight paper cups in a straight line to a tabletop. Fill as many envelopes as you have players with different amounts of the paper squares. Only one envelope should have exactly eight squares in it. The other envelopes should have anywhere from four to 15 squares.

Spread the envelopes throughout the room. Hand out the slips of paper. **Write your name on a slip of paper and put it in this basket.** Hold up the basket. **Let's say our Bible verse together, "A friend loves at all times (Proverbs 17:17)." Let's square off as we learn the Bible verse together. When I say, "Go," that's your signal to scramble to grab one envelope. Ready? "Go."** Make sure everyone has only one envelope. **I'm going to reach into this basket and read the name of our first square-off person. If I draw your name, come up to the table, open your envelope and drop one square into each cup while saying each word of the Bible verse.** You might wish to demonstrate this for the kids. For example, drop the first square into the first cup and say "A." Drop the second square into the second cup and say "friend" and continue on. **When it's your turn, you might run out of squares, have too many, or have exactly what you need. If you have the exact number of squares, you win the big square off.**

Here's the fun part. Before I draw each name, I'll say "Hip-hip hooray, give it all away." That's the signal to give away the envelope that you're holding to a friend. Don't be a square and keep your envelope. After we've all had a chance to use our giving spirit, I'll draw the name of another person to bring his or her envelope up to the table.

Depending on time and the size of you group, you can replace names in the basket to draw again, or have kids who have had a turn step aside. After you have a square off winner, you can play the game again, making sure that there's still just one envelope with the right number of squares.

COACHING CHARACTER
- How did you feel when you had to give your envelope away?
- How did you feel when someone gave you an envelope?
- What makes giving hard to do sometimes? What makes it easy?

Giving is not always easy to do, but it is one way that we can show friendship. God wants us to love each other at all times, no matter what. We give to others because God gives to us. God shows us his love and care and gives to us even though we don't deserve it. Giving shows others that we're God's people. It shows others that we love and care for them even when it might be hard to do.

SCORE WITH SCRIPTURE

A friend loves at all times (Proverbs 17:17).

OUTRAGEOUS OBSTACLE COURSE

STARTING LINE

Create an obstacle course at a park or playground, or set up one indoors with five stations. Clearly number the stations in order. At each station place a shoebox with a word or phrase of a Bible verse clearly written on the front.

1. Jeremiah 17:7
2. Blessed is the man
3. who trusts in the LORD,
4. whose confidence
5. is in him.

On each index card, write a physical task such as: spin around the pole five times, do three push-ups, hop on one foot, etc. Place one in each shoe box.

You'll need to get warmed up to learn this Bible verse. Everyone give me five jumping jacks! Lead the kids in doing jumping jacks.

Divide the kids into five groups. Start each group at one of the different stations. **At your station each of you will follow the instructions written on the paper inside the shoebox. At the same time you're doing the task, you will call out the part of the Bible verse that is written on the box. Finish all the stations. When you get back to where you started, try to say the whole verse from memory, starting from the beginning. If you get stuck on a part, don't worry. Just call out what you know.**

Have the kids go in consecutive order. If they begin at Station 5, then the next station will be Station 1. Repeat at least once, if not twice. Encourage the kids to better their time and their ability to say the Bible verse in unison.

COACHING CHARACTER

• Was this easier the first or second time you played?
• What do you think would happen if you did the course again?
• In what way is this game like real life?

As you repeated the obstacle course it probably got easier and easier for you to remember the Bible verse. As we follow God throughout our lives, it will get easier and easier to trust that he will help us do what is right. The more we learn about God, the more confident we will become. The more confidence we have in God, the more we will be able to do for him. What gives you the most confidence in God right now?

SCORE WITH SCRIPTURE

Blessed is the man who trusts in the Lord, whose confidence is in him (Jeremiah 17:7).

THE GET LIST
• shoe boxes
• index cards
• markers

Ages: 3rd grade and up

Time: 30 minutes

Group size: about 5

Indoor/Outdoor

Activity level: 3

Noise Meter: 2

Godprint:
Confidence

. . . .

USE THIS GAME WITH:

• Mordecai and Esther, Esther 1–9 *(confidence in God's power).*

• Elijah and the prophets of Baal, 1 Kings 18 *(Elijah had confidence as he faced the prophets of Baal).*

TOWEL OF BLABBING ON

Ages: 3rd grade and up

Time: 10 minutes

Group size: medium

Indoor/Outdoor

Activity level: 2

Noise Meter: 2

Godprint:
Resourcefulness

....

USE THIS GAME WITH:

• Jesus feeds the 5,000, Mark 6:30–40 (*Jesus used the resources available to him to feed the people*).

• Joshua defeats Jericho, Joshua 6 (*Joshua had some unusual resources, but God used them to win the battle*).

What can kids learn by being silly with towels? They'll discover that resourcefulness will get the job done.

THE GET LIST
• towels (one for each person)

STARTING LINE

Form a circle with the whole group. Hand out the towels. **Do something with your towel. The only rule is it has to be touching your body somehow.** Examples might be putting the towel on their heads, waving a pattern in the air, wrapping it around an arm or leg, folding and unfolding it. Have all the kids share their actions or motions. Then have the group decide on three favorite actions that the whole group will use and practice them. Ask a volunteer to read 1 Corinthians 15:58: "Always give yourselves fully to the work of the Lord, because you know that your labor is not in vain."

Let's start by going around the circle and having each person say the next word in our Bible verse. If you have more kids than words in the Bible verse, then repeat the Bible verse. You may want to write verse on a board for kids to refer to.

Now let's add a towel twist. As the first person recites a word, he or she will choose a towel action (demonstrate one of the three actions that the group agreed on) **to go with the word. As the player says the word, we'll all do the towel action. Then, the second person recites the second word and chooses a towel action to go with the second word. As we continue around the circle, we'll repeat the towel actions in order as we say the words from the Bible verse. If someone messes up a word or action, we'll start over with the first person and go around again until we complete the circle.**

If your group is quick to accomplish this task, make it more difficult by randomly moving the kids in different positions around the circle. This way they are not always in the same sequence for the word and motion. You can also have the kids use an unlimited number of motions with the towels.

COACHING CHARACTER
• Did the towel help you or make things harder for you to memorize the Bible verse? Why?

Your job in this game was to learn the verse—with the twist of a towel. You had to be resourceful to come up with the motions and to keep up with saying your part of the verse.

• What does being resourceful mean? (*Making the most of what you have to work with.*)
• What does being resourceful have to do with giving yourselves fully to the work of the Lord, as the verse says?
• On a scale of 1 to 10, how fully did you give yourself to the work of learning this verse?

When you work at God's work with all your heart and all your abilities, your effort will never be wasted.

CURRICULUM CENTER
BENNER LIBRARY
OLIVET NAZARENE UNIVERSITY

A Gaggle of Giggles and Games

SCORE WITH SCRIPTURE

Always give yourselves fully to the work of the Lord, because you know that your labor is not in vain (1 Corinthians 15:58).

Kids learn self-control to keep the sand-and their faith-from falling.

STARTING LINE

Fill one zip top bag with sand per team. Cut the poster board into 4" x 36" strips. Write the Bible verse on each sentence strip:" A fool gives full vent to his anger, but a wise man keeps himself under control (Proverbs 29:11)." You'll need one Bible verse strip per team.

Put the kids into teams of four to ten players. Give each team a Bible sentence strip. Then have the team cut the strip into words or phrases so that each team player will have a piece. For example if the team has six kids, they'll need to cut the strip into six pieces.

Give each team a shoebox. Have them put their Bible verse pieces in the box. Put the boxes 20 feet away from each team's starting line. Give the first person on each team a bag filled with sand.

When I say "Quicksand," the first person in line will put the bag on his or her head and go quickly to the shoebox. Keep your hands to your sides. Stay in control, because if the bag falls off your head you'll have to freeze your feet like you're stuck in quick sand. Once you put the bag back on your head you can continue. When you get to the box, take one piece of the Bible verse out. With the bag still on your head quickly go back to your team and tag the next person in line. Then the next person puts the bag on his or her head and moves towards the shoebox. When your team is finished, line up in a row holding your sentence pieces in order. The first team to complete the Bible verse wins! Encourage the kids to remind each other to keep their hands to their sides. You might want to have kids who do touch the bag with their hands before it falls begin again at the start line.

COACHING CHARACTER

• What did you have to do to keep the sand from falling off your head?
• How hard was it to keep your hands from touching the bag on your head? Explain.

You had to control your bodies to keep the sand from falling off your heads. Being in control is not always easy. Sometimes our emotions get out of control. When you're out of control, remember to freeze and let God help you out of the quicksand.

• Tell me about a time when you had trouble staying in control of how you felt.
• Name one way you can use self-control to honor God.

THE GET LIST

• zip-top bags
• sand
• poster board
• boxes
• scissors
• shoeboxes

Ages: 2nd grade and up

Time: 20 minutes

Group size: medium to large

Outdoor

Activity level: 3

Noise Meter: 3

Godprint:
Self-control

. . . .

USE THIS GAME WITH:

• Jacob and Esau, Genesis 27–28 *(Jacob didn't control his own greed).*

• David and Nabal, 1 Samuel 25:1–35 *(David regains self-control with the help of Abigail).*

Remember God is always with you and he is there to help you and to keep you from sinking in the quick sand.

SCORE WITH SCRIPTURE

A fool gives full vent to his anger, but a wise man keeps himself under control (Proverbs 29:11).

POTATO BUD

Ages: 1st grade and up

Time: 10–15 minutes

Group size: large

Indoor

Activity level: 1

Noise Meter: 1

Godprint:
Cooperation

....

USE THIS GAME WITH:

• Ruth helps Naomi, Ruth 1:3–22, 3:1–18 *(Ruth puts her elderly mother-in-law first and helps her out).*

• Paul and Silas in the Philippian jail, Acts 16:23–34 *(Paul and Silas respect the jailer by staying with him when they could have escaped).*

Can a potato teach kids about respect? It can in this game! Kids add parts to a potato-man for each correct answer. As they play, kids learn to respect teammates and the opposing team.

THE GET LIST

• two large baking potatoes
• two plates
• craft foam
• yarn
• scissors
• toothpicks

STARTING LINE

Use the craft foam and cut out two sets of these features: eyes, ears, nose, mouth, bow tie. Cut lengths of yarn, about three inches long. Place each set of features and five yarn lengths on separate plates. Arrange the kids into two teams sitting in circles. Place the potato and plate in the center of the circle. Briefly review the Bible memory verse with the whole group before playing the game. "Always try to be kind to each other and to everyone else (1 Thessalonians 5:15)."

Hold up a potato and a few of the foam features. **This is Mr. Spudbud (or Mrs. Spudbud). Mr. Spudbud is glad to be here today to help you learn a new Bible verse. Your team is going to learn the Bible verse and help Mr. Spudbud at the same time. Let me explain! Each team will start the game by passing Mr. Spudbud around the circle.**

If you're the first player, start by saying the first word of the Bible verse. If you say the right word, reach into the center of the circle and add one item to Mr. Spudbud's face. Use a toothpick to stick it on. Then pass the potato gently to the next player.

The next player has a choice. If you don't know the next word, you can repeat what the player before you said and pass the potato on. Or you can say the next word of the verse. If you add the right word, then you can add something to Mr. Spudbud's face.

The team who helps out Mr. Spudbud by putting all the items on him first is the winning team.

Teams play simultaneously. If you have more time, you can play again and have kids repeat the entire verse in order to add a feature to the face.

COACHING CHARACTER

- What helped you the most when playing this game?
- How did you feel about your teammates who gave a wrong answer?
- Name one thing you liked about the way other players treated you.

Let's say the whole verse together now: Always try to be kind to each other and to everyone else (1 Thessalonians 5:15).

- How hard is it *always* to be kind? Why?
- How does kindness help a group of people working together?

When we treat others with respect and kindness, it's much easier to cooperate. If someone treats you nicely, you feel like working together. And if you treat others with kindness, you'll help them feel like working together with you. We can't do everything without help. We need each other! So let's show each other kindness to make cooperation easier.

SCORE WITH SCRIPTURE

Always try to be kind to each other and to everyone else (1 Thessalonians 5:15).

Kids will learn to work together to accomplish the common goal of organizing the memory verse on the laundry line.

STARTING LINE

Cut the paper into the shape of clothing such as shirts, socks, pants and so on. Write the words of the Bible verse on individual pieces of paper, including the reference: "Then make my joy complete by being like-minded, having the same love, being one in spirit and purpose" (Philippians 2:2). Use the string or yarn to hang a "laundry line" across one side of the room and have enough clothespins for every word of the Bible verse. Scramble the papers on the clothesline, leaving as much space between the items as possible.

THE GET LIST
- clothespins
- string or yarn
- scissors
- copy paper

Ages: 2nd grade and up

Time: 10 minutes

Group size:

Indoor/Outdoor

Activity level: 2

Noise Meter: 3

Godprint:
Cooperation

We're going to hang the laundry out to dry, and hopefully it will never wash away from our hearts! This is how the verse reads from the Bible. Ask a volunteer to read Philippians 2:2.

Now we need to put that mixed-up laundry in the right order, including the reference.

USE THIS GAME WITH:

- The people bring gifts to the tabernacle, Exodus 25:1–9; Numbers 7:1–5; 1–11; 84, 87–88 *(cooperating to bring their gifts to the tabernacle).*

- Psalm 133 *(a psalm about working together).*

Have the kids form a line. **You're going to run, one at a time, to the laundry line. You can move just one piece of "clothing" on each turn. The next person in line gets a turn as soon as you get back and tag him or her. Keep going until the Bible verse words are in the right order.**

The crowd can coach the person as they race a different group or try to beat the clock. Or try the game with no coaching allowed. It will take longer without help from the group!

COACHING CHARACTER

- What was the secret to getting the job done in this game? *(Working together.)*
- How important was it for everyone to have the same purpose in mind? Why?
- Tell me about some other experiences you've had when it was important for the group to work together.

Because we all cooperated and worked together in this game, we're all winners.

- According to this verse, what are three important parts of working together? *(Like-minded, same love, one in spirit and purpose.)*
- What do you think makes working together easy? What makes it hard?

When you hide God's Word in your heart, you're always a winner! And when we are united and work together, we get to the finish line faster!

SCORE WITH SCRIPTURE

Then make my joy complete by being like-minded, having the same love, being one in spirit and purpose (Philippians 2:2).

SONSHINE AND RAINDROPS

Rain a little love on each other by letting kids exchange their favorite Bible verses with this unique twist of an umbrella.

Ages: 2nd grade and up

Time: 15–20 minutes

Group size: 15–20

Indoor/Outdoor

Activity level: 1

Noise Meter: 1

Godprint: *Love*

STARTING LINE

THE GET LIST
- umbrella
- copy paper
- Bibles
- markers
- scissors

- **What's your favorite food?** Give the kids time to respond.
- **What's your favorite sport?** Give the kids time to respond.
- **What's your favorite Bible verse?** Give the kids time to look up a favorite verse in the Bible.

Hand out a sheet of paper to each player. **Let's rain a little love on each other. Everyone cut your paper into the shape of a large raindrop. Then write your favorite Bible verse, including the reference, on the raindrop. Crumple up your raindrop and toss it in this umbrella.** Give kids time to find verses. If necessary, make a few suggestions of verses you think your kids are familiar with.

Open the umbrella and place it upside down in the center of the floor. **God gives us rays of**

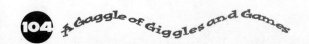

Sonshine and hope in the Bible. We learn about God and about how much he loves us. We learn how to show our love to Jesus and others. **Sharing God's Word with each other and learning God's Word will bring Sonshine into our lives. When I say, "Rain a little love," I want everyone to collect one raindrop.** Spin the umbrella. This should send all of the papers flying. It it doesn't, lift the umbrella up and turn it over.

Now read your raindrop. I'm going to give you about three minutes to try to memorize as much of the Bible verse as you can.

Give kids a one-minute warning when time is running out. **Everyone stand up. When I say, "Rainbow," I want you to start saying the Bible verse that is written on your raindrop out loud.** If kids need to look at their raindrops they can, but try to encourage them to put the raindrops away. **You're trying to find the person who rained a little love on you—the person who originally wrote the Bible verse on the raindrop. When you find the person join hands with him or her.** Everyone should end up holding hands in a circle or "rainbow."

COACHING CHARACTER

• How many of you learned a brand new Bible verse today?
• Give an example of how a Bible verse has helped you with a problem.

God's Word isn't just for reading—it's for sharing! Remembering what God has said helps us when we're in tough situations. Then we can share God's Word with others to help them in their tough situations. Ask a volunteer to read Psalm 119:11: I have hidden your word in my heart that I might not sin against you.

• What does hiding God's Word in your heart mean to you?
• How does having God's Word in our hearts affect our relationship with God?
• How can sharing God's Word show love to other people?

One way to rain a little love in the lives of others is to help them learn more about God. As we memorize Bible verses we learn about God's love for us and others. That's good news that we can share. Share a Bible verse and rain a little love in the lives of others!

SCORE WITH SCRIPTURE

I have hidden your word in my heart that I might not sin against you (Psalm 119:11).

USE THIS GAME WITH:

• Live as children of light, Ephesians 4:17–32 *(being kind and loving each other in truth)*.

•Christ's temptation, Matthew 4:1–10 *(Christ used Scripture to rebuke Satan)*.

RA-RA-REE

Even young kids enjoy cheering for a favorite team. Help your kids put that enthusiastic spirit to work learning a Bible verse with simple supplies.

Ages: 2nd grade and up

Time: 5 to 10 minutes

Group size:

Indoor/Outdoor

Activity level: 2

Noise Meter: 3

Godprint:
Enthusiasm

....

USE THIS GAME WITH:

- Call of Abram, Genesis 12:1–9 *(Abram enthusiastically followed God).*

- Jesus calls disciples, Mark 1:14–20 *(disciples followed Jesus at once).*

THE GET LIST

- brown lunch bags
- index cards
- marker

STARTING LINE

Before class, write the words to the verse on index cards, one word per card, including the reference: "Never be lacking zeal, but keep your spiritual fervor, serving the Lord. Romans 12:11." Place one card in each lunch bag and mix the order of the bags. Have your kids sit in a circle with one or more bags in front of them. If you have more children than bags, you may pair two kids per bag.

How many of you have been to a sports game and remember the words to a cheer you might have heard there? Pause and let kids tell you some of the cheers.

We're going to learn the words of our Bible verse by shouting them out like a cheer. Repeat each phrase after I say it in your most enthusiastic voice! Say the verse phrase by phrase.

Now there's one twist. Each of you has one word to our Bible verse on a card in the bag in front of you. When I say "Ra-Ra-Ree," I want all of you to reach inside your bag, take the card out, and shout out your word as loudly as you can three times like a cheer. Everyone will shout his or her word at the same time. **Here's the hard part: while you're shouting, you also have to listen carefully to what everyone else is shouting out, so you can figure out who has the first word to the Bible verse. When everyone has shouted their words, we'll all point to the person with the first word of the verse, and we'll set that bag in the middle and pass your bags around the circle and play again. Then we'll listen for the next word. When all the word bags are in the center, we'll all cheer out our Bible verse together.**

COACHING CHARACTER

- Why do people cheer?
- Tell me about something that you like so much that you could just give out a great big cheer?

Cheers are a fun way to show our enthusiasm for something or someone. God wants us to be enthusiastic about what he has planned for our lives.

- Who knows what "zeal" means? *(Enthusiasm, eagerness, excitement.)*
- How about "fervor"? *(Same meaning as zeal.)*
- Tell me in your own words what our verse means.

Being a part of God's team and working on his game plan is something we can all be enthusiastic about. You can count on God—he is standing on the sideline of our lives cheering us on.

SCORE WITH SCRIPTURE

Never be lacking in zeal, but keep your spiritual fervor, serving the Lord (Romans 12:11).

BIBLEARY

Use chalk and creative drawing to help remember the Bible verse.

STARTING LINE

Write each of the key words from Psalm 147:8 on a slip of paper: covers, sky, clouds, earth, rain, grass, grow, hills. Put the slips of paper in a brown paper bag. Assign your kids into teams of three or four. For each team you will need an area where they can draw with chalk. **The person in the group who went to bed the earliest last night, please grab the chalk.**

I'll draw a word from this lovely bag. I'll show the word to each person with chalk. When I say, "Bibleary," the person with the chalk will begin to draw a picture of the word the best he or she can. Your team is to guess the word by the picture that your teammate draws. When your team guesses the word, stand up and yell, "Bibleary!" After everyone has guessed the right word, we'll pass the chalk to a new player and I'll draw another word. Now, everyone wiggle your fingers and let your creativity do the talking.

Go to each group and show the player the first slip you pull from the bag. Keep that slip of paper out of the bag. Once all the teams have guessed the correct word, have the kids pass the chalk to new players. Then draw another slip from the bag and show the new person who is drawing the word. Make sure all the kids get turns to draw with the chalk.

When you've gone through all the key words, review then with the kids. Then ask someone to read Psalm 147:8 from a Bible. Have the other kids stand up when they hear a word that they drew, then sit back down again.

COACHING CHARACTER

• Show me the word that your group had the hardest time with.
• What helped you the most when it was time for you to draw the word?

Expressing ideas in picture form is very challenging and really makes you think in a new way. Thinking of things in a new way takes creativity. God is the original creative thinker. Read Psalm 147:8 again.

• What reminders of God's creativity can you find in this verse?

THE GET LIST

• chalk
• slips of paper
• pen
• brown paper bag

Ages: 1st grade and up

Time: 15 minutes or longer

Group size: any

Indoor/Outdoor

Activity level: 2

Noise Meter: 2

Godprint:
Creativity

....

USE THIS GAME WITH:

• Creation, Genesis 1 and 2 (*God created everything and it was good*).

• Psalm 148 (*celebrate God's creativity*).

God thought up everything in the world. He created us in his image, and part of that image is being creative. The next time you have to think in a new way, ask God, the original creative thinker, to give you the creativity you need.

SCORE WITH SCRIPTURE

He covers the sky with clouds; he supplies the earth with rain and makes grass grow on the hills (Psalm 147:8).

GOD IS EGGS-ELLENT!

Kids will get crackin' on memorizing Bible verses by earning points. Watch the points and excitement build!

Ages: 3rd grade and up

Time: 10 minutes

Group size: 2–3 players

Indoor

Activity level: 1

Noise Meter: 1

Godprint:
Diligence

USE THIS GAME WITH:

• The parable of the king's ten servants, Luke 19:11–27 *(we will have to give an account for how we used the gifts that God gave us.).*

• A poor widow gives all she has, Luke 21:1–4 *(giving what you have to God).*

THE GET LIST

• one egg carton
• dried beans
• small slips of paper
• pen
• scissors
• small bowl

STARTING LINE

Cut the paper into 36 small slips (1/4" x 1"). On each slip write one word from the Bible verse: "Whatever you do, work at it with all your heart, as working for the Lord, not for men. Colossians 3:23." Repeat the words from the verse until all 36 slips are used up. Then add one of the following choices to each slip; Add 50 points; Add 500 points; Add 250 points; Add 100 points; Skip a turn; Lose 100 points; Egg cracked, lose 50 points; Give each person a high five; Lose 400 points; Shout out, "God is eggsellent!"; Give a friend 300 points; Get an extra turn; Goose egg 0; Take 200 points from a friend.

Roll up the slips and put three slips in each eggcup. Prepare one set for each group of three or four players.

I have an eggsellent game for you to play with one or two friends. It'll help you get a Bible verse to stick in your eggonoggen. In this egg carton I've put a bunch of slips with words to the Bible verse on them. They also have points for you to add or subtract on your score. To be the top chick or rooster, you must collect enough words from the slips to make the eggsact Bible verse and you must outscore the other player. Hand out the paper and pencils. **Here's some chicken scratch paper to help you keep track of your points.**

To begin play, take turns reaching into the chicken feed and grabbing a few beans. You have to grab more than one bean, but don't grab too many because the game ends when the beans are gone. Drop one bean per eggcup until your hand is empty. Pull a slip from the eggcup you dropped your last bean in. Follow the directions on the slip of paper and add the Bible verse word to your collection. When it's your turn again, grab some more chicken feed. Have an eggsellent time as you learn God's Word. When all the slips are gone, see who has more of the verse and more points.

COACHING CHARACTER

• How hard did you have to work to get the verse done?
• Did you ever feel like you were never going to finish? Why?

• Tell me three words that describe how you felt when you did finish.

How many of you think you can say the verse eggsactly right? Prompt kids as necessary.

• Tell me in your own words what it means to "work with all your heart."
• What's the difference between "working for the Lord" and "working for men"?

I asked you to do something that took some concentration. You had to read instructions, keep score, use the beans, take turns—that's a lot of work. But you kept working steadily until you got the verse finished. Sometimes we feel discouraged about something we're doing and don't really give it our best effort. God wants us to give our best effort to everything we do, because we're working for his glory, not just to please ourselves or other people.

SCORE WITH SCRIPTURE

Whatever you do, work at it with all your heart, as working for the Lord, not for men (Colossians 3:23).

GRIDSOME JOURNEY

What happens when you hurry instead of taking your time? Kids will learn patience and to go slowly as they discover that rushing can lead to mistakes.

STARTING LINE

Use the masking tape to place small Xs on the floor in a grid of four wide and 5 long. Make the marks one foot apart. Set an empty 2-liter bottle on each X. Write the Bible verse in a place where everyone can see it.

You're all about to embark on a gridsome journey as you learn a Bible verse. The object of the game is for the entire group to move through the grid without knocking over any bottles. If someone knocks over a bottle, the whole group starts over again.

THE GET LIST

• 20 two-liter plastic bottles or plastic bowling pins
• masking tape

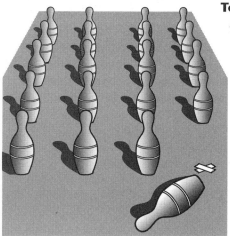

To begin the journey everyone make a circle around the grid. Have the kids walk in one direction around the grid. **When I shout out the reference to the Bible verse I will tag someone. The person I tag shouts out the first word of the Bible verse and then grabs the hand of someone next to him or her. That person then shouts out the next word to the Bible verse and grabs the next person's hand.** This continues around the circle. If there is a large group continue to repeat the Bible verse. **As the group continues grabbing hands the group will also begin their journey through the grid to get to**

Ages: K and up

Time: 20 minutes

Group size: small to large

Indoor/Outdoor

Activity level: 3

Noise Meter: 2–3

Godprint:
Self-control

. . . .

USE THIS GAME WITH:

• Spelunking with David, 1 Samuel 24:4–10 *(David acted quickly and it was not pleasing to the Lord).*

• Cain vs. Abel, Genesis 4: 3–12 *(Cain was not competing with Abel, but Cain's anger caused him to sin).*

the other side. **The first person in line will start leading the group through the grid. Here's a little twist to the game. If I shout out, "gridsome journey," the leader must change the direction through the grid. Remember the goal is to get the entire group through the grid without knocking over a bottle.**

Begin by shouting out the reference to the Bible verse, James 1:19. If someone knocks over a bottle, the whole group leaves the grid and makes a circle around the grid again. Have the group walk around the grid, tag someone else and shout out the Bible reference again. After playing a couple of times, tell the kids to concentrate on encouraging and praising each other.

COACHING CHARACTER

• What kinds of things did you have to do to be sure you didn't knock over a bottle?
• What happened if you tried to go too fast?
• Did any of you think you had a better way to get through the grid?

Going through the grid took a lot of self-control. You had to be careful about how fast you went, where your arms and legs were, and what the people around you were doing. Maybe you felt like rushing or had your own idea about where to walk in the grid, but you had to go where the leader wanted to go. Even the leader could not do just what he or she wanted. The leader had to listen to my voice to find out what to do. The Bible verse gives us some good advice. Repeat the Bible verse together.

• What advice does this verse give for our game?
• What advice does this verse give about our relationships with each other?

We all like to have our own way. But sometimes it's better to use self-control so that we can find out what God wants us to do. That way we can honor God in our actions and our attitudes.

SCORE WITH SCRIPTURE

My dear brothers, take note of this: Everyone should be quick to listen, slow to speak and slow to become angry (James 1:19).

INDEX OF GODPRINTS AND SELECTED STORIES

Abraham 17, 50, 59, 91, 106

Ananias and Sapphira 56

Community 23, 38, 46, 88

Compassion 41, 52, 58

Confidence 99

Conviction 74

Cooperation 80, 90, 102

Courage..11, 78

Creation.................................25, 65, 107

Creativity 10, 64

Crucifixion 27

Daniel....................17, 18, 32, 63, 74, 78

David 8, 12, 17, 26, 36, 37, 48,
..................................53, 63, 66, 67, 70, 82

Diligence..68, 108

Discernment 17

Elijah..29, 74, 77, 99

Enthusiasm 83, 89, 106

Esther.....................................43, 51, 99

Evangelism...21

Fairness 35

Faith...73

Faithfulness 30

Feeding 5,000.......................................100

Forgiveness 27

Friendliness 34, 47, 55, 77

Generosity 56, 98

Good Samaritan 34, 42, 52, 80

Good Shepherd 49

Hezekiah 97

Honesty...94

Hope..9

Humility..25

Integrity 8

Initiative 75

Job 31, 72

Jonah...82

Joseph 36, 62, 65, 72

Josiah 19, 68

Joshua....................................15, 40, 68, 76

Joy..70

Kindness..53

Lord's Prayer 63

Love 104

Loyalty 39

Moses 51, 81

Nehemiah 10, 76, 81, 91

Noah..73

Obedience 20

Paralytic 53

Paul 9,. 71, 72, 80, 82, 85, 89, 96, 102

Peter.......................12, 31, 40, 46, 69

Perseverance 72, 95

Prayerfulness 63

Preciousness....................................43, 57

Prodigal son......................13, 28, 36

Priscilla and Aquila 37, 88

Purposefulness 51

Repentance 81

Resourcefulness 15, 62, 100

Respectfulness....................................40

Responsibility 12, 26

Reverence 19

Ruth.............34, 42, 48, 55, 59, 67, 77, 102

Samuel...95

Self-control....................31, 66, 69, 101, 109

Solomon 15

Stewardship 24

Submissiveness...................................14

Thankfulness 44

Trust..16, 67

Unselfishness..............................79, 93

Wonder..29

Worship 84, 92, 96

Zacchaeus.............................28, 95

INDEX OF BIBLE VERSES

Deuteronomy 6:18	15
Deuteronomy 26:16	21
Deuteronomy 31:6	12
Joshua 24:15	69
1 Samuel 12:20	40
1 Chronicles 29:11	97
Nehemiah 4:6	11
Psalm 23:4	79
Psalm 28:7	71
Psalm 68:35	30
Psalm 86:12	20
Psalm 98:1	83
Psalm 104:24	25
Psalm 118:28	93
Psalm 119:11	105
Psalm 119:18	86
Psalm 119:63	56
Psalm 139:14	44
Psalm 145:3	85
Psalm 147:8	108
Proverbs 3:13	16
Proverbs 12:22	95
Proverbs 15:14	18
Proverbs 17:17	99
Proverbs 25:28	32
Proverbs 29:11	102
Ecclesiastes 4:9–10	35, 78
Isaiah 7:9	75
Jeremiah 17:7	99
Micah 6:8	36
Matthew 7:1–2	53
Matthew 25:21	63
Mark 16:15	22
Luke 12:24	58
John 10:14	49
John 14:1	17
John 15:15	38
Acts 2:44	39
Acts 20:35	80
Acts 24:16	27
Romans 3:23–24	28
Romans 12:5	91
Romans 12:10	51
Romans 12:11	107
Romans 12:12	48
Romans 15:13	10
1 Corinthians 12:27	47, 89
1 Corinthians 13:6–7	68
1 Corinthians 15:58	101
2 Corinthians 5:7	74
Galatians 5:22–23	70
Galatians 6:2	59
Galatians 6:9	76
Ephesians 4:16	81
Ephesians 6:10	95
Philippians 2:2	104
Philippians 2:3	94
Philippians 2:13	52
Philippians 3:13–14	73
Philippians 4:6	45
Colossians 1:16	65
Colossians 3:12	54
Colossians 3:17	90
Colossians 3:23	109
1 Thessalonians 5:15	103
1 Thessalonians 5:16–18	64
1 Timothy 6:18	57
2 Timothy 2:22	67
Hebrews 10:23	31
Hebrews 12:1	82
James 1:19	110
James 2:22	9
1 Peter 1:13	13
1 Peter 2:17	41
1 Peter 3:8	42
1 Peter 4:10	24
1 Peter 5:5	26

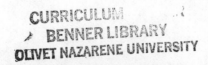
CURRICULUM
BENNER LIBRARY
OLIVET NAZARENE UNIVERSITY